HOW TO BECOME AN EXPERT ON ANYTHING IN TWO HOURS

Gregory Hartley
and
Maryann Karinch

American Management Association

New York • Atlanta • Brussels • Chicago • Mexico City • San Francisco
Shanghai • Tokyo • Toronto • Washington, D.C.

Special discounts on bulk quantities of AMACOM books are
available to corporations, professional associations, and other
organizations. For details, contact Special Sales Department,
AMACOM, a division of American Management Association,
1601 Broadway, New York, NY 10019. Tel: 212–903–8316.
Fax: 212–903–8083.
E-mail: specialsls@amanet.org
Website: www.amacombooks.org/go/specialsales
To view all AMACOM titles go to: www.amacombooks.org

This publication is designed to provide accurate and authoritative
information in regard to the subject matter covered. It is sold with the
understanding that the publisher is not engaged in rendering legal,
accounting, or other professional service. If legal advice or other expert
assistance is required, the services of a competent professional person
should be sought.

Library of Congress Cataloging-in-Publication Data

Hartley, Gregory.
    How to become an expert on anything in two hours / Gregory Hartley and Maryann
Karinch.
        p. cm.
    Includes bibliographical references and index.
    ISBN-13: 978-0-8144-0992-3 (alk. paper)
    ISBN-10: 0-8144-0992-X (alk. paper)
    1. Expertise. 2. Management. I. Karinch, Maryann. II. Title.

BF378.E94H37 2008
001.4—dc22

                                                                        2008020006

Printing number
10 9 8 7 6 5 4 3 2 1

To Rick Croley, my best-read friend and sounding board for enlightening conversation that broadens my mind

— Greg

To Jim, Mom, and Karl, who help me stay authentic

—Maryann

CONTENTS

ACKNOWLEDGMENTS

This collaboration would have never occurred but for Michael Dobson, who pointed out the value of my interrogation knowledge and prodded me to write. Maryann has become not only a good co-author but a good friend along the way. Her voice drives me to explain things in different ways. Dina supports me and keeps me centered, no matter what life throws at me. The publishing staff has been a simple joy to work with. Mike Bosquez has helped to make this easier for me to do along the way. Thanks.

Gregory Hartley

I join Greg in thanking Michael Dobson for bringing Greg and me together. This collaboration with Greg has enriched me in so many ways, I could write a book about that alone. As always, thank you to Jim McCormick, an expert in many areas where I really need expertise, and a source of consistent moral support; to my Mother for her prayers—I appreciate her and them; and to my brother, Karl, whose practical knowledge and personal insights have helped me in many ways. Cheers and thanks to Ellen Kadin for having faith in this project from the start, and to the rest of our amazing AMACOM editorial team, Barry Richardson, Jim Bessent, and Alice Manning. Nods of thanks also to Hank Kennedy, Christina Parisi, and Jacquie Flynn for offering encouragement and provocative questions in the development stages, and to those we have yet to work with at AMACOM to promote the book. Thanks also to David Hemphill for his publicity photographs of me for this book—he and Mary make me smile—and to Spider Spradlin for her illustration.

Maryann Karinch

FLOW OF THE BOOK

Understand the nature of expertise
  and you know why you can become an expert.
Identify the types of people inclined to accept or deny your
    expertise and you see who will open doors or erect barriers
    for you.
Learn to read specific body language
  and unspoken messages will provide cues.
Let who, what, and when guide your planning
  and your preparation will be target-specific.
Design ways to manage information, influence people, and
    display strength and you position yourself to control the room.
Research with precision and limits
    and you will know the terrain without falling down the rabbit
    hole.
Match the style of presentation to your audience's needs and
    expectations and your package of information will suit the
    occasion.
Follow a tried-and-true game plan
  and you will deliver the goods.
Structure options for ending your session
  and the final moments will affirm your expertise.
Learn to swim
  and you will not drown.

INTRODUCTION

THE BASIC WHY AND HOW

¤ ¤ ¤

WHY: THE BOTTOM LINE

Is it worth your time to become an expert? The prestige and privilege associated with being considered an expert seem clear, but doesn't getting there involve a lot of work?

Yes, it's worth your time. Society rewards experts in all kinds of ways.

No, it doesn't take a lot of work if you adopt the process and strategies we describe in this book.

What you will learn here is an ideal skill set for someone who wants to manage people effectively, as well as anyone who needs to forge strong relationships quickly. A *good* manager is an expert on everything. That person understands, "I don't have to know what you know or do what you do to ask relevant questions. I need to know just enough to ask good questions that you can't answer, questions that push you to do things that improve your performance." Or if you're a sales professional, the relevant questions you ask make your prospect conclude that you understand the problems she needs to solve.

In my world of interrogation, I use questions and tidbits of information to convince the source that I know enough to be taken seriously and to make him comfortable so that he will talk to me. I create an ally through the way I use information. In some cases, "ally" means nothing more than a common understanding that we're both soldiers and we're both professionals. I don't presume that I'm going to turn the source into a buddy, but I use information to establish common ground. If I know the same things he knows, then maybe I believe the same things he believes. That common ground gives me more credibility with him than if I came in yelling obscenities and threats. I use whatever facts and images I think will constantly remind him that he's part of the same thing that I am: a military outfit, a family, the human race. In this acute situation, I do what is takes—through a combination of planning and preparation and knowledge of human nature—to be an expert in his eyes.

Many military interrogators have no more than a high school diploma, but they must walk into interrogation rooms around the world and ask questions of experts with very little preparation time. In part, the reason the successful ones can carry this off is a basic understanding of language, behavior, and motivation.

This is what the expert/manager does, for example, and the result is the creation of a bond that makes people want to work for him. Alternatively, he could use his corporate stature to boss people around, showing that he's someone who doesn't care about his employees and demonstrating that by not even trying to connect with their subject areas.

Why would a company want to keep managers like that? Think of the damage they can do. Let's say you have a couple of these committed nonexperts running a service business with a force of skilled employees doing installations and repairs on equipment. The payout to them is $1 a minute if you include both salary and benefits, and there are 1,500 people who receive this amount. If each of them spends three minutes a day complaining about their lousy managers, the company loses $4,500 a day, or more than $1 million a year.

Looks to me as though being an expert means job security—for lots of people.

HOW: YOU'RE HUMAN AND SO ARE THEY

The ability to become an expert in two hours depends first on your knowledge of yourself, and then on your knowledge of human nature. The part of human nature that matters the most is how people perceive themselves and how they relate to others.

What is an expert? Stupid jokes aside, what does "being an expert" mean to you? You must have some description in your head, because it is at the core of why you picked up this book.

We all look for someone who's savvier than we are. It's natural for us to believe that there's someone out there who is smarter, stronger, sexier.

What makes someone who seems smarter, in effect, better than you? Is it your belief that the person has demonstrated more knowledge than you? Or is it something else? In this book, we will help you to answer those questions for yourself and give you a system for developing genuine expertise that has a foundation in human inclinations.

Anyone can pretend to be an expert; in American society, we call people who do this con men. You will not learn how to be a con artist by reading this book. You will learn how to become an expert.

Here's my definition of expert: Think of a complex video game. It wouldn't exist without a skilled programmer, but a 12-year-old aficionado will play it more skillfully than the computer wizard who constructed the line-by-line code. The programmer is the technician; the 12-year-old is the expert. The kid's ability captures the intersection of technology and humanity. This programmer may enter a conversation about the game feeling as though he has the upper hand—until he cannot answer when the 12-year-old asks, "When I pressed these two buttons and moved the joystick, why didn't the guy's head blow off?"

Without question, in order to become an expert, you need to know how to research, what to research, and how to communicate with precision in the time allotted to you. At the same time, your tool kit must include the ability to do the following:

- **Make a connection.** The combination of human connection and value of information imparted is what separates expertise from robotic repetition of facts.

- **Read your audience.** You need to know when someone is buying your information and when he is not.

- **Rescue yourself from disaster.** Tapping into personal interests, asking certain types of questions—there are many rescue techniques that depend on your knowledge of human nature.

- **Terminate the conversation at the right time.** Everyone knows that a half-hour's worth of information delivered in an hour has lots of holes in it.

This book is built on the ability to apply some basic communication tools relied on by first-class interrogators. We will give you those tools and exercises to perfect their use.

In this book, I step you through the process of grasping essentials about human nature, identifying different types of people, assessing to what extent you must plan and prepare for those different types of people, and then presenting yourself as an expert. As a bonus, we give you a solid course on ways out if you find yourself being challenged and put in a corner.

By the way, if you're an idiot, don't try this.

Greg Hartley

1

THE ROLE OF HUMAN NATURE

CHAPTER

1

THE HUMAN SIDE OF EXPERTISE

¤ ¤ ¤

Who was the last "expert" you met? Maybe it was your new doctor. A scientist with daunting statistics about global warming. An army general or even a private just back from Iraq who told you how things really should be handled over there.

What made that particular person an expert? Why did you defer to her at that particular time?

Two common answers would be "knowledge of a subject" and "credentials." The only way such descriptions hold true is if you have broad definitions of those concepts. As you read through this book and grasp the techniques of becoming an expert, you will acquire a perspective on exactly what kind of knowledge and credentials help to qualify someone as an expert.

That's only part of the picture, though. The rest of it involves human nature, including why and how different people perceive expertise. When you can see the whole picture, you will give yourself permission to be an expert.

Let's start with an exercise to help you begin building a tool set to identify human tendencies and understand a few of the things that can make you fail in your attempt to be an expert quickly.

EXERCISE: WHO IS AN EXPERT?

On a piece of paper, write down a list of experts as they come to your mind. They can be experts in any field: religion, politics, finance, movies, and so on. Make three columns. Put each person's name in the first, the subject of expertise in the second, and the person's qualifications in the third.

Expert	Area of Expertise	Qualifications

What if you do not know the person's qualifications? Insert a question mark. (? is a good enough answer, by the way, because it suggests that you trust the person as an expert at a primal level. It's one of the most basic human responses.)

As you go though this book and your daily routine, add to the list. Before you are done, you might even take a few people off as you refine your concept of an expert. You may also add others that you'd never thought of before, including yourself. Do not skip this exercise! I refer back to this list of *your* experts throughout this book.

ORIGINS OF EXPERTISE

The answer to "what makes an expert" is complex and has its roots in elements that have shaped our modern world and continue to do so.

Among the earliest of humans, the "alpha" reigned. Never mind that he didn't know a damned thing more than the others in the tribe: His physical prowess protected his dominant position. He may have delegated authority to those he trusted if it served his purpose, and by endorsing someone, he may even have fully turned over some of his responsibility and authority to that person.

Doing so was a smart move. As the culture evolved, it became more and more difficult for one person to have all the answers for the tribe. If someone had knowledge of when the crops would fail or the animal population dwindle, then he was useful. A bright leader could easily see that endorsing this shaman would transfer to him the responsibility for natural phenomena—and if something went wrong, then the shaman was the one who got the sharp stick in the ribs from angry tribe members. The alpha who knew the power of endorsement was expert primarily at one thing: managing people. His allowing the emergence of the shaman class brought about a kind of power sharing and engendered a specialization of knowledge.

The people who knew why the crops failed obviously understood "the will of the gods," since they could make sense of and interpret changes in the world around them; they became the experts on all things natural and holy. They held the *endorsement* of the alpha because they could interpret the needs of the society and overlay those needs onto their knowledge of the gods. The alpha's endorsement suddenly made them experts. They clung to it and continued to seek it, trying to always know what to say that would please the alpha and drive him to reward them.

As this endorsement took root, an interpreter of the mind of the gods became a new kind of alpha in his own right. The shaman could, on occasion, even say things the original alpha might not agree with. How? By reminding the alpha that he, the shaman, was not thinking for himself: He was the messenger of the gods.

As soon as the shaman had a well-rooted following of those who believed that he was *the* interpreter of the will of the gods, his need for endorsement by the alpha started to fade. The new "expert" was in a position to create his own power structure. Each of the subgroups in this structure then created a system and hierarchy to share power with underlings as the group grew. They shared knowledge selectively with their assistants so that those assistants could be effective at the supportive tasks they were expected to do—like perform a ritual dance—but no more. Those closest to the top coveted the most arcane knowledge, which spawned even more cryptic language and behaviors. Understanding this language and behavior code was imperative for being one of the experts.

In this model of the evolution of expertise, our primate brains, which are ever deferential to the alpha, look for someone who has the knowledge and authority to answer the big questions of life. This transfers into our daily lives in myriad ways.

THE KEY INGREDIENTS

Chimp-like *deference* is the first factor to consider when you are trying to become an expert.

In the beginning, managing secret knowledge was easy; it was accomplished through an oral tradition that was passed on from expert to expert, with the all-knowing head of the clique being the prime repository of information. Sure, you could learn and repeat what he was saying, but the only way to understand it completely and get a stamp of approval was through apprenticeship.

Once in a while, a renegade would leave the organization and share his information, but he could only give away a portion of the secrets because he was not The One, that is, the "all-knowing." Elaborate rites of passage forced an initiate to stair-step his way into the inner sanctum—and even then, he would not command the body of knowledge that The One did. And once he had arrived in the inner sanctum through perseverance, and was enjoying all of the rights and privileges associated with it, what was his incentive to divulge the secrets? The more intricate the *ceremony, language,* or *craft* associated with being The One, the further away from the truth an average person would be, and the harder it was for anyone to approach "expertise." Talk about celebrity.

Each initiate who moved through the hierarchy would get more information and more *trappings* to associate him with the power, and perhaps even more *access* to the seat of power as well. The trappings could be special clothing, weapons, accouterments, or even dialect.

Imagine the impact of the trappings of power if you are a filthy peasant who cannot read or write, and you walk into a majestic stone temple where some guy in spotless white clothing not only can read and write your language, but speaks a magical language of the god. How much deference would that generate? And the people above the initiates have even more intricate clothing and more knowledge, so they must be even closer to the god.

As more and more of the population deferred to these experts, their expertise became a supercultural ability; that is, it expanded past the confines of cities, states, nations, or even continents. In many cases, this expertise became the government of the region, and when it was not the government, it held enough sway with the masses to get the government to do what it wanted. The Catholic Church, for example, had such saturation in Europe that while the average person might never have come in contact with the government in her lifetime, she would certainly have come in contact with the Church. Absolute deference gave these religious organizations absolute power.

A rebel who decided he knew better earned epithets like *heretic* and *infidel*; a whole new vocabulary emerged to describe people who would not bow to the prevailing expertise. Societies often took such a violation so seriously that simply disagreeing with the expert became a criminal offense. In some cases, the person who deviated from conventional expertise became an enemy of the state and was executed. This dynamic of separation for nonconformance underlies a great deal of human behavior.

A DEFINITION SET IN STONE (AND HOLY WATER)

Religious institutions are the foundations of expertise. In European civilizations, they even held expertise in other fields at bay until relatively modern times. Take, for example, the concept of the earth revolving around the sun, or explanations for why certain diseases occur. Why would the experts of holiness care about heliocentrism or viruses? More importantly, why would they care so much that they would threaten to kill the scientists who disagreed with them?

God-centric expertise became, and remains, supercultural. Most cultures on the planet recognize religious experts when they show up. Whether or not you have any idea what the trappings of a particular religion mean, the holistic picture of closeness to The One conveys authority and gives you a vivid picture of expertise.

These people even have titles like "Father" in English and similar names in other languages. They inhabit a role that engenders our trust, as well as our respect, because what they know connects to the meaning of life. One could argue that our deference to religious leaders has left its mark on the psyche of humankind, leaving a similar figure in almost every culture.

I argue the opposite: This need for The One is intrinsic to the human experience. Humans look to these roles to help explain the complex in simple terms. This inclination preprograms humankind for deference to expertise. It explains the allure of a literal translation of the Bible's creation story, which involves no mind-bending theories about the Big Bang and Neanderthals.

OFFSPRING OF THE HOLY PEOPLE

Expertise engenders love, hate, fear, and greed, so it was predictable that religion would not stand alone forever as the institution that shrewdly cultivated a hierarchy of experts. Medicine, law, and science all employ the same techniques. They mimicked religion by using costumes, language, and ceremonies to set themselves apart. The white coats and robes combine with the special words to broadcast the idea: "I know more than you do. It took me a long time to get here." An average person cannot disprove what such experts say because she cannot understand it.

Though most experts in these fields have never held the same power as The One of religion, each restricts access not only to the trappings, but also to power for the few who have been accepted into their ranks.

Movements such as guilds in medieval Europe and unions in later years took the model to the common people and created certification and meaning for the daily work of most people. They added trappings, jargon, and tradition to the way average people conducted their lives. The Guild Hall that still exists in London is a templelike setting that illustrates this point. The more complex and specialized the job, or the more specialized and complex the task, the more expert the certified technician became.

A very short time ago, relatively speaking, the authority of this type of monolithic societal structure started to lose its grip on the rank and file. Starting in Western Europe, where Martin Luther's list of grievances against the Roman Catholic Church was nailed to a church door, this centralized authority that held sway over everyone, including kings, was supplanted. Luther is an example of a modern man who accelerated the evolution of expertise. He convinced Christians that they did not need the papacy in order to gain access to God—a successful argument that resulted in the springing up of countless Protestant groups, which spread around religious expertise, rather than believing that it was the province of a select few. This movement peaked in the founding of a country where there was no church associated with the state.

So what happens when the populist society becomes supercultural and proliferates its ideas around the globe? As a society, you evolve from The One to The Many.

The One was expert on all things. In large part, The One held the power of expertise through intimidation, whether intentional or not. Religious organizations had an audience in the common people and could easily show how much more the initiates knew than the average person. This setup drove the belief that the church must be right, as the church arguably played on our most primate of drives—deference.

This father figure, whether the Pope or the Dalai Lama, interpreted all things in terms of how they affected the lives of his followers. As the power of The One over government, science, and medicine waned, each of these secular institutions gained more power. With the fragmentation of this expertise from The One came the need for expertise in other areas of life.

The institutions of science, medicine, law, and other disciplines that help define modern civilization still have the mimicked trappings of The One, yet the experts emerging from them often prove to be immune to the laws of The One. How powerful does an expert become when he can supplant religious laws, minimizing their role in society by pointing to their quaintness relative to the laws of science, medicine, or law? The irony of the institutions that have been replacing those directed toward The One is that they all use the same techniques to gain deference.

Scientific theories and medical principles replaced gods as methods for organizing the universe and for healing before human beings even discovered the realities of evolution and the function of pathogens in disease. Even now, scientists argue over the origins of humanity and the best way to treat an ulcer, with one faction accusing the other of coming up with voodoo-magic theories. One of the persistent questions in the philosophy of science continues to be, "Is a scientific theory worthwhile if it looks logical on paper, but no one seems to be able to prove it?"

So how are the people mixing chemicals, the people injecting kids with vaccines, and the people with the high-powered telescopes able to assert their expertise? Just like the priests of old, they use jargon, trappings, and access to degrees of knowledge through initiation. These people provide simple answers for complex problems, and we trust them to explain everything from the common cold to conspiracy theories because they are not "just" experts, they are authorities in specific areas.

EMERGENCE OF SPECIALIZATION

The nature of capitalism is the compartmentalization of knowledge: You do something; I do something else. Then we buy each other's stuff for dollars so that we don't have to do things that require us to barter. Capitalism is all about these diverse activities that enable us to acquire and invest wealth, and it requires people skilled in multiple disciplines to create a functional system. The more specialized, complex, and rare the skill set, the more highly the person is compensated.

The more successful a capitalist society is, the more specialized it's going to become. Our educational system is built to produce specialized people. Think of an ant colony. Ants doing different jobs actually have a slightly different physical composition, which other ants sense. Through our educational system, we are doing the equivalent of producing ants with physical differences. The more specialized people become, the more jobs are created. As specialization occurs, though, the more nichelike people's knowledge becomes, so the system of education and employment actually creates barriers to understanding other people's areas of expertise. This *fragmentation of fields of study* engenders deference to people with specialized knowledge.

It's gotten so extreme that average people cannot even understand the implications of what they read, so they go and find somebody to interpret it for them. (I think this is the reason for the proliferation of lawyers in the United States.) Are you one of those people who seeks the interpretation of analysts, commentators, pundits, editorial writers, lawyers, doctors, gurus, and researchers before you will render an opinion on anything? You're normal, but you have to draw the line between experts and specialists or you will be crippled in trying to implement the guidance in this book.

A *specialist* understands every thing about his job. Looking at something holistically is probably difficult for someone like that. If your entire professional day as a medical technician, one type of specialist, revolves around doing sonograms, you can't be expected to advise the patient on what blood test she needs to have.

It's the same thing with doctors, many of whom are classified as specialists. Do you want a psychiatrist to deliver your baby? Most women would wisely choose a police officer over a psychiatrist if they were going to give birth in a taxicab. Firefighters, police officers, and a lot of other front-line civil servants have much more general training than doctors who have earned the title "specialist."

The former are experts. They have knowledge that is relevant to people.

A human being should be able to change a diaper, plan an invasion, butcher a hog, conn a ship, design a building, write a sonnet, balance accounts, build a wall, set a bone, comfort the dying, take orders, give orders, cooperate, act alone, solve equations, analyze a new problem, pitch manure, program a computer, cook a tasty meal, fight efficiently, die gallantly. Specialization is for insects.

—Robert A. Heinlein, science fiction author,
in *Time Enough for Love*

If Heinlein is right, then the civilized world is largely maintained by "insects." While religious institutions were all things to all people, answering the overarching questions about the meaning of life and how everything fit into God's grand plan, the proliferation of specialties is a characteristic of a world with more complex operational requirements. Though the priest may understand how something will affect your eternal life, and even speculate on the origins of the universe, it is unlikely that he can advise you on your 401(k) as well as a CPA.

For a moment, focus on that CPA who helps you, because her expression of expertise is what you're going for here. On first contact with a financial expert, you realize one thing: She knows more than you do. More importantly, though, if she can communicate in a way that makes sense to you, then what she knows becomes relevant to you. Although you were oblivious to her value only moments before you spoke with her, you quickly find yourself being deferential to her because of her use of tools and jargon and her understanding of how the intricacies of 401(k)s affect your life.

Wait: You have access online to information about 401(k) programs. Isn't that good enough to eliminate the need for the financial person? Can't a smart guy like you figure it out for yourself? While in the past, information access was one of the most effective tools used to control expertise, the opposite is true today. The Information Age has brought overwhelming amounts of data into our lives. One person cannot possibly comprehend the significance of all of it. Specialization in vocation breeds fragmentation of information and prevents most people from linking a specific fact or set of facts to the bigger picture. We have experts for that, too. Turn on the morning news or any 24-hour news channel and you find "the experts" in the form of people who specialize in regurgitating other people's words—television news anchors, reporters, and other media figures. As a culture, we have grown to believe that if someone has the knowledge to get into those professions, then he must know more than we do.

We even take this a step further when we see someone affiliated with one of these media stars. It translates into instant credibility. So you trust the knowledge of the private who was in interrogation training for six weeks because he's on CNN—never mind the fact that he was thrown out of the Army before he ever went into the theater of combat. There is never a shortage of disgruntled ex-specialists like this who are "in the know" and willing to share their hard-earned expertise with millions of people for free. (Most people on these programs are not compensated for their appearance.) Producers sort through affiliations as they go "shopping for expertise" to support a point of view.

Expertise by affiliation applies to the whole spectrum of specializations. During media interviews, the hosts of shows are constantly asking Maryann for inside information on interrogation policies and procedures. "That's Greg's thing," she says. "But you write the books with him," they counter.

WAYS TO SET YOURSELF UP AS AN EXPERT

Think back to the list of experts you made at the beginning of this chapter. I told you that putting a question mark under "qualifications" was okay; sometimes, the reason you consider someone to be an expert is simply that you feel that he is. Regardless of why you believe in that person, his expertise revolves around the formula he uses for making facts intersect with people.

Any of these formulas wraps together subjective criteria, such as how smart the person appears to be to a particular audience, and more objective criteria, such as how much information that person has. As I go through the categories, loop back to your list once again and use these categories to describe how the people on that list expressed their expertise.

Some of the ways in which people can become experts require action, while others are passive in nature.

PASSIVE

The two categories are isolation and affiliation.

ISOLATION

After receiving the benefit of Army training, I know a lot about edible plants and how to find water, as well as general first aid and survival medicine. I also grew up poor, relying heavily on common sense and country intelligence. So if you and I were stranded like Tom Hanks in *Cast Away*, which person would you trust more to save you: me, or the botanist you met on the plane just before the crash? Depending on how specialized his knowledge is, the botanist may or may not be able to tell you what plants have potential as food, but it just so happens that a survival-trained soldier can do a whole lot of things to help you survive. Isolation creates expertise by paring down the list of competitors.

AFFILIATION

Although there can be an active component to this, affiliation is often a passive means of establishing expertise. Consider the general who also comments on the nightly news. He has two affiliations: He became a general in a very competitive professional military, and he has the endorsement of the evening anchor or he would not be commenting. Let's say that pundits attack this general. His retaliation is that he reminds the audience he was a member of the Joint Chiefs of Staff and served as an adviser to President X. He has now actively validated himself though affiliation. Someone who works in a doctor's office must be more able to give medical advice than an auto mechanic because she is "in the business." Or as a good friend of mine in New Jersey likes to point out, everyone in Princeton is intelligent because they live in the shadow of the university.

ACTIVE

Unlike affiliation and isolation, to show expertise through the following means a person always needs to do something.

DEMONSTRATION

The expert shows what he knows and how that is important to your life; this can be tangible skills or an understanding of complex concepts, like those of the CPA who helps you plan for retirement. This can play out in many ways though the use of strategies we will explore in later chapters, particularly in Chapter 5.

ASSOCIATION

The person takes information that is otherwise useless and relates the information to something that you already know. This anchors the idea in your head and makes it part of your repertoire. I will do this throughout the book by calling on symbology and archetypes to make abstract information part of your cache of knowledge. This will help you get a better grasp of the information than you would have had if you had gotten it without these anchors. Association gives you the ability to tie this information to many aspects of your life. Think about how you were taught geometry: If all you learned were theorems, your eyes would glaze over. As soon as you realized that you couldn't build houses or bridges without knowing geometry, it got more interesting.

GENERALIZATION

The expert using this technique presents complex concepts in basic pieces. She makes the information make sense by taking it to the lowest level that has application to your life. A neurobiologist could tell you that your autistic child has a higher gray-matter-to-white-matter ratio, but that's meaningless until you understand how that translates into an ability to collect data, but not process connections.

HUMANIZING

Take any topic—technology, weather, politics—and make it about the human experience. The media successfully do this on a daily basis by telling you what impact a Gulf War has on the price of gas for your car, for example. (I'm not saying they're accurate, but I am saying that this is a great example of humanizing.) You can't understand why r22 refrigerant should be replaced in HVAC systems? A humanizing expert will quickly help you to understand that the seas are going to rise and destroy X amount of beachfront property and make the beaches uninhabitable when the ozone is depleted by Freon as it leaks from your household air conditioner. (Note: I deliberately used mind-numbing jargon here.)

ADAPTATION

Move the conversation from a topic that seems to be diving down the rabbit hole to one that is more easily understood by all. Tom and Ray Magliozzi do this brilliantly on their NPR show *Car Talk* when the know-it-all launches into a question about compression ratios and they translate the jargon into a problem that any horse-and-buggy driver would appreciate. By doing this, the expert-through-adaptation brings the conversation around to a point where everyone can contribute to it, or at least understand it on some level.

INTIMIDATION

Experts with this technique use trappings, language, ritual, or facts that others are not privy to and drive home the point that they are among the privileged and should not be questioned. This is often the shakiest of grounds for expertise, but the hardest for most people to combat.

THE DEFINITION OF EXPERTISE

Once again, go back and review your original list of experts. Can you now replace some of the question marks with the categories discussed here? Maybe some of these experts who got a question mark are regular folks in your life, like a teacher or your grandfather. Do you now understand how your fifth-grade teacher, Ms. Jones, who had no distinctive clothing, no Ph.D., and no seniority in the school system, could become one of your experts?

EXERCISE: THE WHY OF EXPERTISE

Flip through a news magazine. Each time you see the name of someone you consider an expert, connect the person with the categories just covered.

Some teachers reached you. Others bored you into doodling and daydreaming. What was the difference? The teachers who engaged you with information made it relevant to you, like the CPA who advised you on your 401(k). Those who didn't spewed facts that probably meant something to them, so they thought all that stuff should mean something to you as well. They made little or no effort to connect the information to your life. You might call both types of teachers experts, if only because "expert" has become a title, as I mentioned in relation to designations like "Father" or "Pastor." In the sense that we use "expert" in the title of this book, however, only one type of teacher qualifies as an expert; the other is a human encyclopedia with information flowing one way in a standardized format.

You can't become a priest in two hours, but you can become Ms. Jones or the CPA who makes a difference in your life. You're about to find out how.

You have started your journey in learning to use the process interrogators use to become an expert. A basic understanding of human behavior is the key to becoming an expert (as opposed to pretending to be an expert) in two hours. In the subsequent chapters, you will learn to read people better than you do now, to prey on the human drive to defer, and to use these skills to become invaluable in a broad array of situations. You will also learn to give yourself license to be an expert.

CHAPTER

2

DEVELOPING YOUR SKEPTICISM

¤ ¤ ¤

Human beings want to believe almost as much as they want to belong. Blame the Internet for aggravating this tendency. What began as a communications device quickly morphed into a mechanism for packaging total fabrications as historical evidence, research, and news.

All of the following have been "reported" as fact on the World Wide Web and in print media. Which one is true?

- Microsoft founder Bill Gates will pay you anywhere from $400 to $1,000 to forward an e-mail as part of an "e-mail tracking system."

- Senator Hillary Clinton once refused to meet with a delegation of Gold Star Mothers, women who had lost sons or daughters in military combat.

- There is evidence that man never actually landed on the moon.

- A 1950s experiment with subliminal advertising in a movie theater proved that this type of advertising worked because of the on-the-spot jump in sales of Coca Cola and popcorn.

Answer: None of these statements is true. But I'm willing to bet that you believed at least one of them because you:

- Had read it in, or heard it from, a so-called trusted source.

- Don't like the person or the product.

- Found it comfortable to embrace a simple explanation of a very complex concept.

- Had heard or read it so often that it must be true.

Do not beat yourself up for having an inclination to believe what you read or hear. Cynics make lousy company. What you must learn to do in order to become an expert, however, is to develop skepticism as part of your skill set and have confidence that most of the people you encounter in life will believe what you tell them as long as it sounds reasonable.

Maybe you passed this skeptics' test with a perfect score. You might simply be a well-informed person who looks for multiple angles on the news. Do you hang on to that sense of doubt when it comes to the following?

- Do you believe that people have the ability to direct *chi*, or life force, in a way that gives them the ability to fight with greater power? Examples would be some martial arts experts who assert that they can control the flow of this energy.

- Do you believe that some people can control pain and the rate of healing when they mutilate their bodies because they have a way of channeling energy from a holy leader to themselves? Examples would be Sufi mystics and Indian "miracle men."

- Do you believe it is possible for people who have mastered certain meditative practices to fly, even briefly? Examples include yogi flyers and St. Teresa of Avila.

These are three of the phenomena explored in the National Geographic episode "Superhumans," part of its *Is It Real?* television series. Ostensibly, the investigators pursuing the facts proved that, no, you cannot direct *chi*, channel energy from one person to another, or defy gravity. What the episode demonstrates more powerfully, however, is how much the mind of a believer will "make it true."

No number of skeptics with tools for scientific measurement and degrees from major universities will shake the faith of a true believer. You may be thinking, "I never fell for any of those things!" Fine; then try these undocumented "truths":

- Do you believe in Virgin Birth, a concept embraced by Christians, Muslims, and pagans?

- Do you believe in an afterlife? Does it apply to people only, or will your dog go to heaven, too?

- If you're Catholic, do you believe in transubstantiation, that is, the miraculous transformation of bread and wine into the body and blood of Jesus Christ during the Mass?

- If you have the money, will you make arrangements to cryopreserve your body in preparation for a day when you can be brought back?

The range of possibilities you have in your desire to be accepted as an expert runs an astonishing gamut, doesn't it? Essentially, you can have a lock on some people when your expertise connects you with a higher power or paranormal phenomenon. But you can also move people into the believers' circle quickly based on how trustworthy you and your sources seem, how simple and "logical" your explanations are, and how familiar your facts sound. Science has its own version of this: If I can show you a preponderance of evidence to support my leap of faith, then you would be an idiot (infidel) to doubt me.

Have you heard of string theory, that model in physics that says that the little bits of the universe aren't really zero-dimensional point particles at all, but really strings of stuff? Think you need help understanding it? Consider this commentary by Jim Holt in his *New Yorker* article "Unstrung" (October 2, 2006):

> *Dozens of string-theory conferences have been held, hundreds of new Ph.D.s have been minted, and thousands of papers have been written. Yet . . . not a single new testable prediction has been made, not a single theoretical puzzle has been solved. In fact, there is no theory so far—just a set of hunches and calculations suggesting that a theory might exist. And, even if it does, this theory will come in such a bewildering number of versions that it will be of no practical use: a Theory of Nothing. . . . String theory has always had a few vocal skeptics. . . . Sheldon Glashow, who won a Nobel Prize for making one of the last great advances in physics before the beginning of the string-theory era, has likened string theory to a "new version of medieval theology," and campaigned to keep string theorists out of his own department at Harvard. (He failed.)*

So when is your doubt skepticism and when are you simply being a contrarian? We can step toward the answer to this complicated question by looking at the circumstances when skepticism is healthy and when it is not.

HEALTHY VERSUS UNHEALTHY SKEPTICISM

Skepticism falls into two categories: healthy and unhealthy. Let's look at both when they've been in play.

As privileged, ambitious, and smart as he was, investor Warren Buffett tried—more than once—to get a job with his mentor Benjamin Graham's firm. He believed that Graham's investment expertise surpassed his own, and he committed himself to learning everything he could from Graham. The results have made Buffett legendary, not only in the financial community, but in history. That is an example of healthy skepticism as an element of reflection, or self-analysis.

Dr. Jonas Salk, who developed the vaccine that halted the polio epidemic, showed a healthy skepticism about the prevailing medical wisdom. He didn't buy into what his med school professor said about how to counter a viral infection, and that doubt ultimately led to the first effective attack on poliovirus.

Contrast these stories with the saga of Britney Spears, who started questioning the abilities of everyone around her. The result was a devastating blow to her career. She did not know where her limits were and how she could expand those limits, but she didn't seem to care. Concluding that she was enough of an expert about her career that she could fire professionals, as well as trusted companions, who handled publicity, contracts, hair style, and other areas of her life, she let her deformed skepticism about their expertise put her on a fast downhill slide.

She demonstrated what many CEOs have demonstrated in the past: Just because you have achieved a great deal of respect and/ or popularity through your accomplishments in one area of your business does not mean that you have a right to this response in other areas. An inflated sense of your own capabilities, combined with a string of failures, can engender a paranoia that "it's their fault." In Spears's case (I'm speculating), the pervasive doubt about other people's ability to help her made her truly desperate for a guru. Not finding any gurus where she was hanging out (i.e., nightclubs), she turned to herself. The outcome is going from expert to fool.

A more common scenario is unhealthy skepticism about one's own abilities. One of the greatest benefits you may get out of this book is ways to uproot that feeling. Understanding skepticism as it applies to you will equip you to identify and deal with the skeptics you will face.

TYPES OF SKEPTICS

Certain types of people are naturally skeptical, and others cultivate skepticism because of their role within an organization.

Generally doubtful people might be categorized as *contrarians*. The word *contrarian* is jargon from the world of finance that has found its way into common American usage. The term originally described investors who defied the prevailing logic. This spotlights a basic point: Just because someone does not agree with the majority does not mean that he is wrong. This was brought home clearly in the fable of the Emperor's New Clothes, in which the one person to "get it right" was a child who bucked what every else was saying by blurting out, "But he has nothing on!"

Contrarians challenge everything from single statements to conventional wisdom with a new theory. A man revered by the tribe might have observed a fruit tree in springtime and declared: "Look at that tree. It died several moons ago, and now it has come back to life better than ever. That is reincarnation." The contrarian beside him observed the same tree and said, "No. It died because the gods were angry, and now it has come back to life because we once again pleased the gods."

Contrarians have been responsible not only for debunking the assertions of experts, of course, but also for refining their theories. Those experts who felt secure in their knowledge accepted the new ideas and challenges and built on them; those who felt threatened sometimes fought back with invective or even violence. This was the sentiment of Roman Catholic popes when faced with contrarians like Martin Luther and Galileo.

This means that contrarians are a sort of natural skeptic. They are born to question. This does not mean that they have the facts right or are anywhere close to correct in their perceptions. The world of contrarians is littered with idiots in equal proportion to the world of the gullible; they just have an opposite predisposition.

My label for the natural skeptics is "threshold thinkers." You do not have access to their trust or their full attention until you earn it. Threshold thinkers are hard to win over, but once you do win them over, they are your greatest allies. Commonly, when other people observe that you've proven yourself to a threshold thinker, then you automatically gain their acceptance, too.

In the context of an organization, one or all of these types of people may be inclined to doubt you before you've said a word:

- **The natural leader.** This person may or may not be an expert, but people are deferential to him because of his role.

- **A genuine expert.** This is the person who is most knowledgeable about a particular subject, probably the subject of the meeting.

- **The loud guy.** Habitually spouting off, he is constantly trying to convince people that he knows more than he does.

For a number of reasons, each of these types of people might be skeptical:

- **The natural leader** has a vested interest in ensuring that what he endorses is correct. If he cannot separate himself from the incorrect information by insulating himself, he loses his hard-won status. In the case of a formal leader, he may even lose his job. In addition, he may have reinforced his reputation by standing by a genuine expert in his group. Does he have a compelling reason to invalidate or dilute the expertise of that person by endorsing you? This dance to gain his acceptance is a complicated one.

- **A genuine expert** has most likely invested considerable time and resources in establishing her credentials. Whether she obtained them because she has been the best problem solver, has demonstrated an understanding of issues that are important to the group, or has a relevant academic background, none of this has come easily. Why should she freely roll over and hand you her title? This person has the most to lose, because if she openly endorses you and is wrong, she loses. If she defies you and is wrong, she loses. If she endorses you and is right, only through careful management can she save face. The complexity of your relationship with the genuine expert gets more thorough treatment in later chapters when I cover specific applications of your new skills. The key to success in this dance is achieving some degree of mutual admiration, but the danger is that the new alliance can alienate others who see it.

- **The loud guy** simply spouts information that he has heard or believes. Probably through sheer persistence, he has gained some renown as an expert. In most cases, he will be expert in isolation; as a refresher, I noted in Chapter 1 that isolation creates expertise by paring down the list of competitors. While the loud guy is dangerous to you in his role as a skeptic, the minute he becomes convinced that you are the genuine article, he becomes even more dangerous. He cannot lose his grip on the tenuous expert role he has created and thus will go to great lengths to discredit you. This is the person that you do not want to become, but that you risk becoming if you cavalierly apply only bits and pieces of the information in this book! The loud guy does exactly what you do not want to do: He comes in unprepared, armed with nothing more than attitude. When he sees a threat in the form of someone who projects more knowledge than he does, he reacts with a vengeance.

Your first task in coming across as an expert with a group that contains all of these types of people is to figure out which one of these people will be your biggest skeptic. The more you know about the particular self-interest that motivates each type of skeptic to doubt, the better able you will be to cultivate trust as needed.

Here are a few options:

- With the natural leader: Generally speaking, it's a bad idea to irk him. Try to match what you know with what keeps him awake at night. In other words, find his pain and help him out, rather than try to impress him.

- With the genuine expert: If you succeed in becoming *the* expert, then the most knowledgeable person loses her status. However, if what you say supports her, then she is validated by another expert and goes up a notch.

- With the loud guy: Neutralize him by focusing on the natural leader and the genuine expert, but don't overtly try to shove him to the back of the class.

You need to play the role of skeptic in order to sharpen your ability to detect disbelief.

2

PLANNING AND PREPARATION

3

BODY LANGUAGE OF EXPERTS, CON ARTISTS, AND EVERYBODY ELSE

¤ ¤ ¤

When you want to become an expert in two hours or less, you have three primary reasons for developing skills related to reading and controlling body language.

First, you need to know whether or not other people accept you as an expert. You will detect when the skeptic in the group is a threat to your credibility and when he reaches his threshold of acceptance.

Second, you will discover ways to adjust your body language to avoid any suspicion that you are uncertain about your own presentation of expertise.

Third, armed with these new insights about posture, movement, energy, and voice, you will cultivate the skill of using these pieces of body language proactively to get the desired acceptance from all but the most discerning of eyes. As a corollary, this is a skill of con artists, so you will be equipped to spot them. (Reminder: This book is about becoming a real expert—someone who has substance to offer—not a con artist. Whether this substance is adding value to a conversation with someone who would have intimidated you in the past or solving a real work-related problem, you want to genuinely add value and not become the office joke, or worse.)

We could summarize the three categories as follows:

- Detection

- Protection

- Projection

DETECTION

I will take you through a crash course in reading individual movements using a head-to-toe scan, and then analyze body language holistically. You can use this knowledge of body language to detect how someone perceives you in the role of expert. The observation skills you develop will help you to know whether or not she:

- Rejects you.

- Is undecided.

- Accepts you.

In terms of someone else's expertise, you will learn to detect either confidence or uncertainty.

Some pieces of body language are unintentional and simply tell you what the person you are talking to is thinking. Other pieces can be used intentionally to signal a specific message. The most interesting aspect of human body language is that even the tools we use for intentional messaging can betray us and send clear, but unintended, messages about our innermost thoughts. I will briefly discuss these to give you tools for detecting them, and then teach you to protect your own messages and project what you want others to see.

Since this is not a book about body language (as our previous one, *I Can Read You Like a Book*, is), I will just touch on several of these indicators. You will need to hone these skills related to body language as part of your preparation to become an expert, but they will also serve you well in myriad other circumstances, such as negotiating, selling, or flirting—you name it.

BODY LANGUAGE BASICS

Every human culture has unique signals in body language, or *gestures*. Thumbs up and fingers in a "V" are accepted indicators of "it's good" and "peace," respectively, in modern American culture. Throughout the book, I will use "movements that capture meaning within a particular culture" as an operative definition of *gesture*. These are moves with agreed-upon meanings; they capture a concise thought and are used quite deliberately.

Among the other elements of body language are the basic four used by humans to communicate what they are thinking, either intentionally or, more importantly, without intent: *illustrators, barriers, adaptors,* and *regulators.* Unlike gestures, few people can identify this form of communication, and even fewer understand it. Yet on a gut level, many people are able to spot incongruities between words and message.

Your ability to identify each element not only will help you read other people much more clearly, but will also allow you to use body language to support your presentation of expertise.

Illustrators are the brain punctuating its thoughts. Illustrators can be hand, head, eye, or even foot movements. Anytime someone uses a part of his body or an extension of his body to emphasize or elaborate on a point, you are seeing an illustrator. Think of the last time someone rolled his eyes at you. That is an illustrator. The kind of whipping arm motion, or batoning, that President Clinton used in his denial of having had sexual relations with Monica Lewinsky is a prime example of an illustrator.

When people are not being deceptive or under some other kind of high stress, their words are generally punctuated by their bodies; brain and body are coordinated on the message. Watch politicians: When their hands and arms seem too big or out of synch with the message, you might subliminally think, "That's weird. Why don't I believe her?" Conversely, when you believe an actor and get into the moment of a TV show, you feel the congruence of words and gestures; together, they draw you toward the message—and the person. *Illustrators can be intentional or unintentional.*

Adaptors are outlets for a person's stress. Fidgeting, shuffling, nail biting, and picking at fingers are all examples. People use ritualistic grooming and self-petting of every type to relieve nervous energy. This category of body language is the one that is most likely to become idiosyncratic, and therefore the toughest to describe. Just realize that whenever a person does something to relieve stress, you are seeing an adaptor. *Adaptors are rarely intentional.* Only people who are well trained in body language are self-aware enough to use this most complex of signals to their advantage.

Regulators either encourage someone to continue speaking or control who gets to speak. The most recognizable of these are cultural, and everyone recognizes them—signals such as pressing a finger to the lips, or holding the finger in the air and rotating the hand to signify "wrap it up." Mothers and preschool teachers tend to use exaggerated regulators such as the zip-the-lip move. *Regulators are typically intentional, but they are used so often that they can become unintentional*; that is, they become somewhat ritualistic. For example, someone who is accustomed to regulating conversation at the family dinner table by pursing her lips may inadvertently do that in a meeting when she wants people to shut up.

Barriers are protections from threats, either real and tangible or representative. Most people use a barrier of some kind when they are nervous. For example, both intentionally hiding behind the podium and holding a laser pointer in front of the body represent a thin line of protection from the "enemy." They block observation of you, so they prevent your stress level from rising, thereby negating the need for adaptors. *Barriers are most often unintentional.*

A PRIMER ON INDIVIDUAL BODY MOVEMENTS

In this head-to-toe scan, you need to focus more on baselining—determining what's normal for someone—than on memorizing the meaning of individual actions. There are lots of human beings out there with "normal" twitches, as well as a host of neurological conditions that profoundly affect how people use their bodies. Be smart: Do not judge someone on the basis of an isolated movement unless you know for sure that it is a universal *and* involuntary movement, and the difference should be clear from the following descriptions.

EYES

Eye movements can clue you into the thought process going on within a person's head. The eyes follow an easily readable pattern. By asking a few simple questions, you can determine that pattern for an individual; you learn how the person's eyes move when he is engaging specific parts of his brain. You can not only know when he switches from fact to conjecture, but also pick up clues to his specific emotional state.

I'm not just saying that the questions *can* be simple, by the way. I mean that they *must* be simple; those are the questions that work best in this exercise.

Remember the urban legend that we use only 10 percent of our brain? The truth is, we use most of our brain, with different portions dedicated to different tasks. Observing eye movements helps us to understand which part of her brain a person is engaging at the moment. This means that the questions need to be simple in order to engage one section of the brain at a time and create a baseline for that person. Then we can look for deviations from that baseline, or normal pattern.

The visual cortex is at the back of the brain. When you are thinking about something you have seen or are visualizing, your eyes will drift up, often looking above the brow ridge.

Right now, take your eyes off the book and remember your third-grade teacher's face. Where did your eyes go? If you are like most people, your eyes not only went up, but also went to your left. With your access to memory showing up as a look to the left, your memory of an image pulls your eyes to the memory (left) side of the visual cortex, which is located in the back of the head. Up left is a default setting for visual memory in approximately 90 percent of the population.

The portions of your brain that process sound are located directly over the ears, so in recalling or creating a melody or noise, your eyes will drift toward your ears, usually between the brow ridge and the cheekbone. Again, 90 percent of us store memory on the left side, so our eyes will look slightly up and to our left when recalling a sound. Try it now: What is the last thing you heard on the radio? I have never seen a person who remembered visually to the left and auditorily to the right, so once you have memory for auditory cues, you also have memory for visual cues.

Cognitive thought, internal voice, and problem solving occur in the frontal lobe. When you are calculating or analyzing, you will find that your eyes, and maybe even your whole head, move down and to your left. Moving down and to your right corresponds to intense feelings.

Figure 3-1 gives you an overview of the mechanics of analyzing eye movement.

When you are dealing with a supposed expert who is really just a con artist and you ask him to recall factual information, you

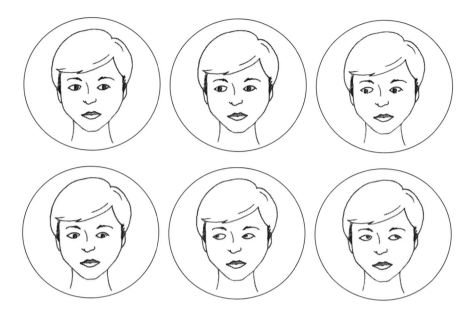

Figure 3-1. Eye Movement Diagram.

will notice eye movement to the construct side of the brain, even though a real expert would be recalling information. That observation alone will boost your confidence in countering this person directly, or simply moving the conversation in a direction of your design. More importantly, as you ask and answer questions, you can begin to notice people internalizing what you are saying. You will see whether you have triggered someone to remember something related (up left), ponder what you just said (down left), or have an emotional response to your comment (down right). You can use this skill set to know whether you have just made a connection or pinged the BS meter.

FACE

Brow movement can be a strong indicator of acceptance, disbelief, or uncertainty. And when you pair certain brow movements and mouth actions, you have portraits of very specific states of mind.

An initial, involuntary, and universal response to recognizing a person or an idea is the eyebrow flash. By flash I mean a momentary rise, rather than an exaggerated raising and holding of the brow. You see someone you know on the street, and you do it automatically. You hear a concept that rings true, and you are likely to do it as well. This sign of affirmation can tell you, the expert, that you have hit the right chord.

The lack of it can signal the opposite. Let's say you run into someone from high school and don't remember her. She instinctively realizes this if you look at her blankly; on a subliminal level, she picked up the fact that you did not signal recognition. The same kind of thing happens when people discuss issues. A familiar or welcome point of view or idea will spark that same eyebrow flash. If you do not see it, you might well wonder if your audience doesn't believe you, or if what you said isn't connecting with anything the audience members know or care about.

Combine an eyebrow flash with a smile up to the eyes—a real smile in which the muscles near the temple crinkle—and you go beyond mere acceptance to genuine approval.

Now if you take the downturned sides of the mouth, which usually indicates disapproval, and add the brow rise with animated eyes, you get the "who-woulda-thunk-it" look.

The grief muscle between the brows often unintentionally sends messages as well; you can eliminate that problem with Botox injections. Disbelief, confusion, and/or fascination also show up through this kind of brow action:

- Wrinkled brow

- Knit brow

- Arched eyebrow

- Two arched eyebrows (also see the discussion of the "request for approval" later in this section)

Combine a wrinkled or knit brow with a drawn mouth or the corners of the mouth pulled downward, and you have some serious disbelief or even disgust. Combine any one of these with a smile and you have someone you've driven to lunacy.

People convey uncertainty with a look that I call "the request for approval," which involves two arched brows, often with either a drawn mouth or a tight-lipped smile. President George W. Bush executed this during many speeches with something that I call a goofy country-boy smile, as if to say, "Y'all believe me, dontcha?"

In addition to the brow, women have a nose gesture that also sends a clear message of disbelief, disapproval, or confusion: the crinkle. I'm convinced that whenever men do it, it's learned behavior, but it's perfectly natural for women.

The mouth sometimes operates all on its own, too, in ways other than not knowing when to shut up. (I address that later.) If you were presenting yourself as an expert, what would people think if they saw you biting your lip? Or pursing your lips, as if you were holding back emotion? You can control those gestures once you're aware of what they project, but here's something that you cannot control: swelling. When you are attracted to a person, blood flows to the lips, cheeks, and other areas of the body that are involved in seduction. Let's say you've done a great job of project-

EXERCISE: MIRROR, MIRROR

Do the movements I just described while looking at yourself in the mirror. In addition, have a friend do them that so you can sharpen your sense of what the positive and negative expressions can look like.

ing expertise—so great, in fact, that you rule the room. To both genders, that can be very sexy.

Before leaving the face, think about what many people do with their jaw when they are tense, uncertain, judging, or calculating. They clench their teeth. Raising the chin to a higher level than normal can indicate indignation, and it rarely indicates anything but a negative reaction to the stimulus.

This is just a primer on the face, but these tools should serve as a good foundation for understanding what you are seeing.

LIMBS

Arms and legs make lots of involuntary movements to relieve stress (adaptors), but they also help you emphasize a point (illustrators), shield you when you want separation or distance from someone (barriers), or attempt to exercise control over a conversation (regulators). They also help you convey your mood, your response to a situation. Fingers and toes serve the same functions, but more subtly. Think of the judge regulating the arguments in her courtroom by steepling her fingers to indicate, "I've heard enough. Get on with it or I will make you stop talking"(regulator). Or the speaker with stage fright who curls his toes the whole time he's presenting his research (adaptor).

If you have ever watched a tree in the wind, you can understand why a human's limbs are such powerful indicators. Just like tree limbs, people's arms and legs typically flail more violently and demonstrate more than the torso does. Add to this the fact that we use our arms and legs on a regular basis—they have residual or "muscle" memory for things we usually do—and you realize how difficult masking their messages is.

Most illustrating and regulating are done in concert with conversation; this is a good starting point for understanding why illustrators and regulators are the most expressive movements. But humans, "the tool users" who have complete command over so many implements, have a hard time controlling the two tools they were born with—the hands. Our hands receive much of our focus from our first moments of consciousness, with most people looking at their hands many more times per day than they look at their own faces, and yet we have a much harder time describing them than we do our faces. This separation from our most basic tools allows them to do work that is rarely intentional.

Most barriering done by the hands involves an adaptor as well, so that when a person is hiding behind his hands, he also wrings his hands as if washing them to relive stress. For women, a normal barrier with the hands is to place an extended finger across the throat or chest as a protective measure. In true female fashion, a woman relives energy in a much more subtle way than a man by tilting her head and smiling.

Hands are great for creating adaptors as well. Human beings groom and fidget with them in times of stress (adapt), pushing back the cuticles of their nails, rubbing out an imaginary spasm, or simply rubbing the hands together. We also use these first tools to signal everyone around us to get a word in edgewise (regulate). The ways we use our hands to send messages, whether intentional or not, are innumerable. I've mentioned just a few to open your eyes to the signals that are all around you, including the ones you are sending right now.

When the hands move, the arms are the drivers, so while some-one may learn to "sit on her hands" at a meeting, she will rarely learn to hide the guarding, flailing, or petting that are typical indi-cators of what is going on in her head. Crossing the arms means nothing as an absolute, but when this form of barriering accompa-nies a stressful topic, it is an indicator of the need for a shield. When this is not a person's standard behavior—something that you would have picked up in baselining—it can mean a desire to be away from the situation, topic, or person. This might occur, for example, when you first start talking with a "real" expert. He assumes that you know very little about his topic and begins the conversation with his arms folded and a slight smirk, eyes slightly closed, and a dull conversation tone. As you begin to demonstrate your understanding of the topic, he becomes more animated, uncrossing his arms, opening his eyes wide, and raising his brows. Aha! You are in.

When I first moved back to Atlanta, I met a self-impressed young woman at a party. She asked what I did for a living; I told her "project manager." In polite form, I returned the question, "What do you do?" Raising herself to her full height, she said I probably would not know much about what she did. "I have a master's in psychology, and I work in a stress laboratory." "I might know more than you think," I told her, explaining some of the stress responses I had seen in interrogations. Her body language morphed steadily as the exchange continued, starting with an offensive posture—closed and arrogant, eyes partially closed, arms illustrating her superiority—as she declared, "You cannot have seen that! We cannot reproduce those results in the laboratory!" And later, as she listened, she showed some openness and receptivity. But as she was unable to meet my challenge that what she did was playing, whereas what I did was real, her body language became barriered, with arms across the body. The more she realized that I applied things that she had only read about, the more protective she became.

Women can also use their arms to cover the abdomen as the ultimate sign of stress. Think of the fig leaf and the abdomen cross as two of the most protective stances that people take. The fig leaf is hands folded over the genitals, or it may be hands holding papers or something else, to "protect the precious." Men from different cultures and in diverse situations use this signal of uncertainty. It could well be a subtle signal that someone feels threatened by what you're saying. And if you do this while you are presenting, then you broadcast uncertainty. The female version of this is covering the abdomen with the forearms in a barriering posture. I have noticed this when teaching young women in the interrogation field in the past, and I have often called it "egg protecting." Most young women balked at this until I became more verbally aggressive and approached closer to their space, causing them to assume the posture. This always brought a laugh from the class.

Always keep in mind that the baseline is all-important. What you think is discomfort may just be standard behavior, but you won't know for sure unless you know what a particular person does normally. If your normal posture is egg protector or fig leaf, though, you need to fix it. It broadcasts insecurity.

That said, some combinations of moves are so extreme that they would rarely be classified as "normal." Placing the hand in front of the genitals with crossed legs is very likely a closing-off, defensive move. And consider the message a person sends when he crosses his legs while doing something extreme to control the animation of his hands—like sitting on them. Does he start to show the desire to get away, or controlled energy around a topic? Either sign can indicate that he is overriding his desire to regulate the conversation and get that word in edgewise. The legs have some of the most powerful muscles in the body, and energy escapes as an adaptor constantly.

VOICE

Not only what you say, but also the way you say it can change the pace and tone of communications and indicate acceptance or rejection.

When you see a tilt of the head that suggests acceptance, ask yourself if the voice is strident, lyrical, coarse, or breathy. Stridency means that the vocal chords are tight; it could be that that's how the person always talks (remember to baseline), but if this is not normal for her, then it's a sign of stress. If someone suddenly goes from strident to lyrical, and her normal speech is strident, then you might have a problem—or an invitation. Someone who deliberately softens her voice could be baiting you, or she could be hinting that you're doing okay.

The key point is that a noticeable change in vocal character indicates a change in state of mind.

READING THE FOUR BASIC MOVES

Each of the categories of basic moves (illustrators, barriers, adaptors, and regulators) contains indicators of rejection, indecision, and acceptance. Some of the moves stand alone as signs of a person's reaction to a situation or statement, but others convey their real meaning only when combined with particular facial expressions.

Even facial expressions used by humans to send an intentional and clear message carry a different meaning when stress alters the expression. What happens when stress ramps us up? The body says one thing and the mouth says another. The increased adrenaline and cortisol production triggered by stress cause blood to leave the skin, which makes the lips thinner than normal and the cheeks look a bit drawn. It's the opposite of the flushed, plump-lipped sexy look caused by blood flowing to the mucosa in a state of arousal. Other stress signs are that the pupils dilate to take in more information about the perceived threat and breathing is shallow and rapid. Often, a furrowed brow and a few adaptors will be added to the picture.

After the following discussions on general signs of what an accepting, undecided, or rejecting image looks like, I'm going to introduce you to characteristics of moods, such as surprise and disapproval. This is a holistic approach to reading body language that encompasses intangibles such as energy and focus, and the genesis of it took shape as Maryann and I were writing a book devoted solely to that subject. For you, we took this new system of evaluating the meaning of a set of physical and vocal elements and interpreted it to help you learn to become an expert quickly. You will explore specific moods in relation to expertise.

ACCEPTANCE

General

A genuine smile, rather than the toothy grin of a jackass eating briars, nearly always indicates that the person accepts you. This kind of real interest shows in the eyes as alertness and bright recognition. Generally the person is focused on you, and the pupils may dilate slightly to take in more of a good thing. The pupils should not be extremely dilated, however. Pinpoint pupils indicate disinterest, and dilated pupils typically indicate sexual attraction or rage.

A mood in which the person's energy is high, the focus is on you, and the direction of the energy is clear—that is, all the arrows are lined up in one direction—is also a very good sign. You see openness and fluidity. When you see the same profile of energy, focus, and direction, but the movements are closed, jerky, and accompanied by stress, however, you have definitely alienated someone.

Illustrators

You are looking for openness and fluid movements. Hands, arms, and eyes all indicate a relaxation with your presentation, or an animation that openly encourages you to keep talking. Elbows up and hands raised in a kind of "yes" or even "hallelujah" is a combination that gives you a strong sense of acceptance, particularly if it is paired with a genuine smile. The approving person may even start to move his hands to illustrate your words when he really gets it and accepts your ideas as his own.

Adaptors

A person who accepts you has a certain comfort level with you, so that either you will not see adaptors, or they will be minor things that might relate to the fact that your expertise is a bit intimidating. When you do see adaptors, if they are accompanied by good, positive energy and focus toward you, they can be nothing more than a way of bringing your earth-shattering insights into the listener's brain. Think of the lottery winner smiling as he rubs his hands together, contemplating the many ways to spend his newfound millions.

Barriers

Making no attempt to close you out and removing barriers, whether real or figurative, signals acceptance. This is one more way to convey openness, which is the fundamental character of acceptance.

Regulators

Watch television show hosts such as Chris Matthews, Bill O'Reilly, and Oprah Winfrey when they want someone to continue to talk. They relax their body language to give it a nonconfrontational appearance. They nod "yes" and may even motion to the subject of the interview to keep talking. This positive use of regulators indicates that you are agreeing with what is being said and understanding.

UNDECIDED

General

Undecided movements and vocal responses range from timid, questioning expressions to downright challenges, depending on the source. (Keep this in mind for later, when you want to take someone down a notch.)

On the pastel end of the spectrum, you see brow action that indicates questions and attempts toward openness, which are described later in greater detail. At the other extreme, hands on hips is defiant; it's a challenge. Coming from someone who's listening to you, it might mean, "Really? I probably know more than you do about that subject." You've gone from pastel signals to a red alert.

Illustrators

Go back to the Clinton example. If he had opened his hand while batoning, you would not have felt the same way about his denial. The gesture would have had a more suppliant quality. If someone did this to you in a conversation, you would probably get the sense that she wants more information from you. Imagine the fingers extending and curling as she speaks, as if to say, "Help me to understand this."

Adaptors

What immediately comes to mind when you hear "*The Thinker*"? Hands on or near the chin, eyes cast down and to the left? Rodin's sculpture captured this in such memorable detail that it stands as the consummate representation of someone in deep thought. This adaptor of placing the hand to the mouth or chin, along with others, such as stroking the hair, can indicate that the person is adapting new information to an existing schema. Watch yourself as you try to understand the impact of the new information you are getting from this book. When someone is taking your information and mulling it over, he is deciding whether it is true and where it fits inside his head.

Barriers

Most people will give intermittent signals on whether you are trusted or not as you approach their threshold of acceptance. Among the best is steepling, that is, holding the fingertips together in an upright position. Typically, this is a protective move to keep the person separated from you until you show value. When the fingertips rotate forward to a horizontal position, you are winning the person over. In general, look for barriering followed by dropping and maybe even reestablishing the same barrier as the person weighs the merits of accepting you as a trusted source. The movements might become more extreme if the options are "trusted source" or "kook." Think of a flirtatious toddler when meeting a new person: Hands over the face; hands down. Grabbing your shirt one second; pushing you away the next. Adults are just old toddlers who learn routines to cover most of that extreme behavior.

Regulators

The person may show a mix of head shaking and nodding as she interprets your value. The more positive the regulator, the better you are doing. If you start off being accepted and then see more negative regulators creeping into the person's repertoire, you are not doing well, and you may need to change your delivery to get her to understand you.

REJECTION

General

You are looking for the opposite of acceptance movements: those that are closed, halting, and bored.

Illustrators

People don't whip you out of acceptance; they whip you out of rebuke, frustration, or disgust. So when you are in conversation with someone who browbeats you, moves his arm like Hitler giving a speech, or shakes his head—all whipping motions—you know that you have not won him over.

Another illustrator of rejection is a movement that figuratively pushes you away. If you've ever had a disagreement with someone across a desk or at the dinner table, you've probably seen the action of both hands sliding toward you on the surface. That's one of the obvious examples.

Adaptors

Depending on the relationship you have with a person to whom you're presenting expertise, adaptors can be pronounced as she tries to overpower her natural instinct to verbally disembowel you or throw you to the wolves. People who have the upper hand will typically have reserved adaptors because they feel very little stress; they may, in fact, grin at you, with the combination of movements producing a decided threat posture. Those who feel outright uncomfortable with what you are saying, but are not in a position to cause you damage, are likely to adapt dramatically, as they feel uncomfortable for you. Usually adaptors will be controlled and may even include a sense of amusement in representation.

Barriers

The classic barriers come into play when you are rejected outright. Things such as turning away from you, crossing arms or legs, and placing physical objects between the two of you are signs of discomfort or outright disdain. You are dismissed.

Regulators

Typical regulators used by people rejecting the speaker have to do with discouraging the speech. Head shaking, the head looking up in exasperation, and even exhaling can all be nonverbal ploys to ask you to shut up.

Table 3-1 summarizes what to look for.

THE BODY LANGUAGE OF MOODS

The system is a kind of flash-card (anyone remember those?) method of pegging the moods or mental states that surface when someone is either struggling to convey expertise or evaluating an expert's presentation. In addition to giving you specifics on body language, this system gives you a holistic look. It definitely does not serve as a substitute for the preceding discussion; in fact, it incorporates an understanding of that more detailed view.

This holistic approach to reading body language is not something that interrogators are taught. I developed it in teaching body

Table 3-1.

	Accepting	Rejecting	Undecided
Illustrators	Openness and fluid movements; casual and friendly	Whipping and pushing motions; pointed, directed, and concise	Palms up as if asking for help or other punctuation that is a question mark
Adaptors	Few or none; when adaptors are present, they support an overall positive message	In those with less power relative to you, they show up as utter discomfort; in those with more power, they are a controlled complement to displays of amusement	Moves associated with concentration or contemplation
Regulators	No signs of wanting to interrupt you	Moves that say, "Enough"	A mix of "go on" and "what the—"
Barriers	Down	Up	Intermittent; should go from up to down

language to people who need to read it in a normal (not a prisoner-of-war) setting.

In analyzing these moods, I use three criteria: energy, direction, and focus.

1. *Energy.* By energy, I do not mean that the person is necessarily happy. Energy can come from agitation, too. How much life does the person appear to have in her? Does she look as if she could not take another step, or as if she is sitting on her hands to prevent herself from going out of control?

2. *Direction.* The person might have high energy, but is she like a squirrel in the road, or is she directing her energy at a

target? Do all of her arrows align with getting something accomplished, or is she just giddy, with energy spraying in all directions? In one case, the direction is sharp, and in the other, it is scattered. As with specific pieces of body language, with a mood indicator like direction of energy, you must look for what is normal. Sometimes, even intelligent people can stay on track for only two sentences at a time.

3. *Focus.* Is all of that energy, whether scattered or directed, concentrated internally on an issue or externally on a stimulus? The difference is whether the primary attention grabber is inside the person's head or somewhere else. Focus alone is a good indicator of mental state.

SURPRISE

Surprise is a high-energy mood that can be either a good or a bad sign. The focus is clearly external, provoked by something that has happened in the environment, so the energy is sharp, going straight toward the person or thing that provoked the mood. The look of surprise is a straight-up lift of the eyebrows. It can be a good indicator if the previous body language you saw hinted at rejection; the person may now be intrigued by what you're saying, so you have a chance to win her over. On the other hand, if you saw all the signals of acceptance, and now you see surprise, this could mean that you have just given the person information that he did not expect. Now you need to pay attention: Does his body language indicate that he accepts, rejects, or is undecided about your new data?

DISAPPROVAL

Disapproval is a low-energy mood, but again, the focus is external and the energy is sharply directed at someone.

Outright disapproval has some clear facial and body signals associated with it, but the energy is not the demonstrative behavior of someone who is angry. The corners of the mouth turn down. A woman will crinkle her nose. Sometimes just touching the nose means that a person is disgusted, but the gesture will differ from a stress gesture. It could be a wipe with the back of a hand (when there's no reason to wipe), or a finger against the nose. This is not always bad for you. Look for the cause of the disapproval. You may not be in danger; in fact, you may use this knowledge to discern whether the object of the person's disapproval is also your natural enemy or one of your skeptics. Remember: The enemy of my enemy is my friend.

Suspicion

Understanding the appearance of suspicion is an absolutely necessary survival technique. In suspicion, the energy is low but sharply directed, and the focus is external. By low energy, I mean that the person is not demonstrative, but the energy that is present is sharply directed at the object of suspicion; he is under high scrutiny.

The squinty-eyed listener with brows down tight is displaying misgivings about the expert's assertions. Squeezing one eyelid shut can also express extreme disbelief. A less harsh version is partially closing the eyelids as a barrier to further conversation or contact. And then there is the person who combines a raised brow with a jaundiced eye and a slight smirk—you can bet you have a credibility problem with her.

Confusion

With this mood, energy is low, direction is scattered, and the focus is internal. Whereas in suspicion, the combined elements mean, "I understand, but I think you are a con man," confusion means that the person simply doesn't get what you're saying.

You'll see a knit brow, and possibly regulators that indicate "slow down" or "repeat that." The person's voice may have some stridency because tension is present. Often illustrators will not emphasize the right points because the brain is out of synch with the body. Confusion can be a start down the path to rejection if you don't address it; conversely, if you catch it early and mitigate it, you pull the confused person closer to acceptance.

The expert who suddenly becomes so preoccupied that he may not even notice anything else is suffering from confusion. His mind has discovered something that threatens his very being at that moment. This saps his energy, and his body language exhibits an incongruity in his picture of the universe. He starts to drown. It could happen to you, too, but don't worry. I give you rescue tools in Chapter 10.

DISTRACTION

This is a high-energy mood, with the direction scattered and the focus internal.

If you don't command a person's attention, you have not gotten her acceptance. Her body language is discordant, not sending a unified signal. The mind of a distracted person has an overwhelming preoccupation: "I'm hungry." "I'm late." "My head hurts." "This is boring." This fixation prevents the person from focusing on anything else—unless that something else takes on a greater urgency than the cause of the distraction. Do not try to compete with that cause with a louder, funnier song and dance. Say what you think the person needs to hear and move on. The real key here, as with most other moods with an internal focus, is that you are battling for attention against a private show going on in the person's head. Most of the time you will want to get him out of that show and back to yours. In some cases, however, that internal focus is good for you. For instance, getting the skeptic or contrarian to lose track can often prevent him from attacking you. When he finally realizes that he's missed key points you've made, he will look foolish if he says anything critical.

Anger

You probably don't need an expert to tell you that anger means rejection. This is high energy, directed sharply at you and caused by you. The energy is so high, in fact, that it will seep out no matter how hard the angry person tries to conceal it. In this state, the consuming passion is getting rid of the source, whether figuratively or actually. Look for signs of this.

Watch for displays of aggression, even restrained ones such as illustrators with a closed hand and regulators that punch out the sentiment "shut up." Rigid and concise moves serve as weapons.

Typically, when people are rejecting you with the force of anger, their sentences become shorter, the voice is strident, and their posture grows stiff. People who are not contrarians by nature will become contrarians when angry. Nothing you say can be valuable when you are the source of someone's anger.

Secretiveness

Secretiveness is a low-energy mood, but because there is a specific reason for it, the person has sharp direction and external focus aimed at guarding the secret.

If you've provoked this response, you could well be in trouble. Look for the target of the person's focus. Maybe she knows that the leader of the group has a master's degree in the subject you're addressing and that you are well on your way to looking like a fool. If the target of her secretiveness is someone else, you may have a tool that you can use. When someone has a secret, she often has a hard time keeping her eyes off of the affected party. You will notice adaptors and barriers—the antithesis of the openness and fluidity that signal acceptance. Secretiveness involves a lot of contained energy, so the adaptors may even take on the look of fidgeting. If someone has all the earmarks of secretiveness, but stays focused on herself, it is a precursor to embarrassment.

EMBARRASSMENT

A low-energy mood, embarrassment involves energy that is directed sharply and internal focus on the source of the problem.

People don't expect to feel embarrassment, so their movements are often awkward. You can expect to see adaptors and barriers, as well as flushed ears and cheeks. All of these are figurative means of escape.

If you caused this embarrassment unintentionally, you are likely to move from approval to rejection. You should be aware that when you use embarrassment intentionally to get the upper hand, you should meter the acceptance of others in the room to know whether gaining the upper hand at someone else's expense will work or will backfire.

CONDESCENSION

This is another low-energy mood. As with disapproval, the focus is external and the energy is sharply directed at someone.

Remember when your ninth-grade history teacher looked across the bridge of his nose when you answered a question? You knew at that moment that something about your answer was wrong. Depending on the critic's facial structure, this can be a very predatory look; at the very least, it indicates condemnation. The target is the key. If you are the target, you have a problem, but if the target is someone else, you just may have an ally. You need to choose: Will it serve you better to build a bridge or to dig a chasm?

If the answer is a chasm, you need to decide which side of the chasm you belong on.

CONCERN

Concern has the same profile as surprise, and like surprise, it can be a sign of a tendency toward either acceptance or rejection.

A straight-up lift and use of the pain muscle—the muscle between your eyes that Botox paralyzes—is often paired with sympathetic eyes. If you see open and encouraging illustrators, then the concerned person is on your side. When the barriers go up, the concern may be migrating toward disbelief and rejection.

Now that you have some basic tools for categorizing moods, give yourself permission to start cataloging these and others. You will use them not only to predict outcomes, but also in the self-defense strategies I cover later.

PROTECTION

Experts need to be certain. As you look at the body language pointers just given, all of which describe moods that can change quickly, depending on people or situations, you begin to understand that people's bodies send clear messages about what is in their heads. And moment by moment, what's in someone's head can change.

If you doubt this, go out for a walk. Contemplate the most negative things you can remember for just a few minutes. As you do this, pay attention to your body language. Your gaze, and often your entire head, will drift down and to the right. And then, as a result of accommodating the shift of 11 pounds of dead weight, your posture changes. If you prefer not to bring yourself down, try thinking happy thoughts and watch your pace quicken and your energy increase.

The body language of certainty and confidence is solid posture, with eyes engaging the audience and the body punctuating your thoughts with illustrators. You reduce barriers to a minimum or drop them altogether because you don't need them. Your body language is open and fluid.

The negative body language I described is as self-evident as the positive. You have just never seen it codified in writing before. What I want you to get from these anatomical descriptions of moods is the precise knowledge of how you can protect yourself even when you feel insecure and tentative. At the same time, you will know how to project an air of confidence. Protection involves blocking negative signaling, and projection is a proactive move to send out the message that you are in control.

The body language of helplessness, uncertainty, and desperation figures prominently here, because when you manifest the deferential gestures associated with these moods, you are losing ground with your audience. You don't want to use these gestures even when you are trying to suck up to the true expert or the natural leader to get him on your side. You need to avoid body language that makes you look weak or confused, such as a request for approval, steepling downward, or obvious adaptors such as shuffling your feet or rubbing your neck.

Here is an overview of how to protect your own signals.

POSTURE

Extreme movements are indicators of discomfort. If you are a ladder-backed former Marine, then standing rigid and motioning with arms extended is typical for you, and it's what people have grown to expect from you. Not only is it indicative of your confidence, but it is also your baseline. If a shy new dishwasher in the cafeteria suddenly did the same thing, it would be an indicator that something was different. She might be attempting humor, or she might be trying to broadcast confidence. The point of having erect posture is not to exaggerate it for the purpose of sending a signal. The point is to maintain what is good posture for you and not show the rounded body language of helplessness or the stiffened back that indicates uncertainty and the need to be perceived as powerful. Be fluid and comfortable to avoid sending the message that you have been waiting for this opportunity your whole lifetime.

BARRIERS

Almost everyone sets up barriers to some degree, whether it is sitting behind a table or rubbing her hands together. Take note of your own baseline on this one: Learn how frequently you set up barriers when you are in a relaxed state. If you set up barriers constantly, practice reducing your reliance on barriers incrementally. When you are pitching yourself as an expert, that will noticeably improve your presentation because using minimal barriers shows that you have confidence in what you are doing. I am not advising you to step away from all barriers, though, unless and until that becomes a perfectly comfortable state for you. Doing something dramatic like that will make you feel unsafe, and that will show. By paying attention to the how, when, and what of your normal barriers, you will learn to use them effectively and deliberately. If you always sit behind a big desk, move to something smaller and practice transferring nervous energy through your feet by curling your toes. No one will notice unless you're wearing sandals.

ILLUSTRATORS

Illustrators are the mind punctuating its thoughts regardless of the mouth's intent. When you broadcast a message of expertise with your mouth, but your brain is uncertain, your illustrators will give you away.

The brow raise that I call a request for approval is an undeniable help-me indicator, showing that you are uncertain of how you are being perceived. Avoid it unless that is the message you are trying to send. Similarly, other illustrators of helplessness and uncertainty are hunched shoulders, palms up with fingers extended, and elbows close to the side. These all indicate a loss of control and dilute the image of confidence.

In addition, avoid illustrators such as batoning that send the message that you are beating information into the audience in a Hitlerian fashion. And whatever illustrators you use, make sure that they hit key points rather than seeming like robot arms flailing after a power surge. Some of the best instructors I have known in the military rehearsed consistently to get this emphasis correct.

When we are in a relaxed state, most of us (unless we have stabbing pains or neurological conditions) move our arms and legs fluidly, without choppy movements. Our cadence of mood shifts and emphasis coincides with the message instead of rushing to the next step. Glitchy and choppy movements indicate preoccupation and lack of comfort.

Do whatever it takes to ensure that the message your hands and arms are sending supports your words. This is likely to happen when you are sure of your information, but at the first bit of uncertainty, your brain will sabotage itself. Guard against this by not rambling.

REGULATORS

People who are in charge control the conversation through the use of regulators. Experts often allow others to contribute when appropriate, and exclude their comments when it is not appropriate; both are done through regulators. Once you take control, you can use regulators effectively to incorporate ideas into the discussion or exclude them from it. Use the regulators that are already in your repertoire rather than trying to adopt someone else's. You would look foolish in a business meeting shutting someone down with Dr. Evil's "talk to the hand" regulator. Protecting your idiosyncratic gestures that indicate that you are asking for approval to proceed is an absolute must. For example, if you have a tendency to put your finger to your lip as if to shut yourself up (as opposed to the reason why your mother did it), then put your hand somewhere far away from your mouth. You have permission to speak as long as you have something to say.

ADAPTORS

This is the single most demonstrative indicator of stress and uncertainty for most people. From giggling with nervous energy during a presentation to drumming your fingers to twirling your hair, you are fidgeting your way to rejection. There is no more certain way to lose credibility than to put out this rubbing, shuffling energy refuse that shows that you have no confidence in your delivery. (Extrapolation: You have no confidence in your substance, so why should anyone else?)

The first thing to do is learn what your indicators of stress are. The best way to do this is to put yourself in a new and uncomfortable situation to learn what you do to adapt to that new environment. If you don't usually go to church, then go to church. If you don't usually go to the opera, then go to the opera. If you don't usually show up for a pickup game of basketball, then do it. You have to learn what you do when you're tense in order to mask those signs. While most of us do not know our own adaptors, we notice others' quite readily, so while you're doing your little experiment, learn something extra by checking out other people at the church, the theater, or the playground. Assume that those around you have watched you and know your adaptors, and learn to protect them. In summary, it's not only the holistic body language of moods that can sabotage your success. The basic four elements—illustrators, adaptors, barriers, and regulators—indicate your shifting degrees of certainty and uncertainty as you speak. Choosing to allow others to see your true thoughts is powerful when you are confident. Controlling your unspoken messages with the use of these same tools greatly expands your options for presenting expertise.

PROJECTION

In a strict sense, projection means that you see what you want to see. I use it here in a slightly different sense: You are going to project to another person how you want her to respond to you. Using the basic four elements, you can send messages that you want others to see. And especially in a one-on-one situation, you can also learn to emulate body language to get more cooperation and respect.

To start, look at how to use some of the basic four offensively.

ILLUSTRATORS

You can use the brow lift to request approval—when you know you're right.

The normal perception is that you are asking, "Do you get it?" or "Do you believe me?" If you see concern in response to this gesture, you can clarify your point to help others get it. If the person watching you is a skeptic and thinks that he sees weakness, he will see this as an opportunity to attack. You counter by clarifying your position; you know what you're talking about.

Controlling your use of illustrators to provoke questions that allow you to rise up is a great ploy—or a fantastic way to boost your credibility. While you do not want these signals of uncertainty to creep in when you actually are uncertain, planting them to elicit questions that you can answer is a masterful use of body language.

Illustrators that are strong and fluid drive belief. Build into your plan, and even practice, the moves you can fall back on so that you can punctuate your points.

ADAPTORS

Adaptors almost always show weakness. The best offensive use of adaptors is to signal weakness in your areas of strength to invite others to question you. It's analogous to the use of the request for approval gesture when you have no need for approval.

Overuse of adaptors will nearly always ensure rejection unless they belong to a mirroring strategy, which I discuss later.

BARRIERS

Move out from behind the barriers, but do not sacrifice comfort for openness. Seeing you tethered to a podium is much less disconcerting to others than watching you cough, shuffle, and stutter on a bare stage. Go just one measure beyond what people expect from you, and they will see confidence. Go just one measure beyond what you have usually done before, and you will invite yourself to grow into a more confident state.

REGULATORS

Use inclusive regulators that draw others in. Positive moves such as nodding to keep someone talking work well as long as you don't look like a bobblehead doll. The more others have contributed to your success, the less likely others are to attack it.

MIRRORING

Mirroring encompasses the basic four elements—and much more. It involves using the body language of others to endear yourself to them. This does not mean aping their behaviors. It means getting the gist of what someone is doing, perhaps picking up a modified version of his adaptors, illustrators, and cadences. This works best when done in a small meeting, or even a one-on-one session.

CULTURAL NORMS

Cultural norms also encompass the basic four elements—and much more. You have to play on what others believe to be so when it comes to using the body language of an expert. So, if the popular notion is that crossing your arms suggests the need for protection—and therefore projects uncertainty—then even though you know that this is not necessarily true, you have to bow to that popular misconception.

Sample gestures, and the common American perceptions (which are actually misperceptions) associated with them, include:

Crossing arms	Uncertainty; the need for distance
Knitting brows	Confusion, uncertainty
Sustaining eye contact	Honesty, confidence

People believe these meanings, so use them proactively.

APPLICATION

Humans communicate on more levels than most people know. Commonly, we think of communication as involving words and movement, but the realm of "words" can include umms and errs, as well as countless variations on pitch, tone, and cadence. And understanding body language starts with knowing what people do normally—and how big a range is that?—and goes all the way to their physical responses to extreme situations.

The more familiar you become with the range of human communication, the more you will be able to identify signs of acceptance and rejection. Using your knowledge of body language, you can also guard against sending the wrong messages, and even pro-actively engage the skeptic.

Understanding how human beings generally respond to exper-tise, and how they naturally twitch and bitch when they either accept or reject information, gives you the setup for success in your quest to be an expert.

4

THE DRIVING FORCES—WHO, WHAT, WHEN

¤ ¤ ¤

Your audience, your desired outcome, and the duration of the session determine the nature of your planning and preparation, from what you plan to wear to how you say good-bye.

- Who are you talking to?

- What are you trying to accomplish?

- How long do you have to do it?

The answers to these questions shape my preparation for every interrogation, for which I have to become an expert on any number of things in two hours or less. Your answers to them are the driving forces behind your ability to be an expert just as quickly in a business or social environment.

YOUR AUDIENCE

Expertise comes from your audience. If you do not have an audience, it doesn't matter how smart you are or how many facts your brain has stored. You are a voice in the wilderness. Part of becoming an expert, therefore, is having an audience, and then understanding who it comprises. This audience then drives your decisions about what to learn and how to apply it.

How smart do you think it would be for an American interrogator to begin his preparation for an encounter with an Arab source by reading everything he could about Hamas? Obviously, it makes no sense unless he's certain that the source has something to do with Hamas. Only after you identify your audience can you establish what its members need to hear from you in order to consider you an expert.

There are two main ways to categorize your audience: focus and motivation.

Here are examples of how, based on knowing the focus of an audience, a politician can do a good job of tailoring his presentation for his audience:

In a speech delivered on October 26, 2002, in Chicago at Federal Plaza at an anti-Iraq war rally organized by the ANSWER (Act Now to Stop War & End Racism) Coalition, Barack Obama said, "Now let me be clear—I suffer no illusions about Saddam Hussein. He is a brutal man. A ruthless man." He then went on to assert that "Saddam poses no imminent and direct threat to the United States, or to his neighbors."

At a political fundraiser in Houston, Texas, on September 27, 2002, George Bush personalized the description of Saddam and the direct threat for his audience of supporters: "After all, this is the guy who tried to kill my dad."

Obama knew his audience: a defiantly left-wing group led by intellectuals. Their perception of his competence would likely be aroused by an expansive and subject-specific vocabulary; they would be wowed by Barack Obama and his Ivy League lexis. (How's that for a Harvard word?) Similarly, President Bush hit the mark with his audience, who expected something more down home. By referring to the personal threat of Saddam Hussein, he got the message across with no frills, just unadorned language with a story attached. Being an expert does not mean sounding like

Barack Obama if the audience calls for someone who sounds like George Bush.

Both politicians—and the best ones understand and act on this—succeeded for a corollary reason, and it's a fundamental part of being an expert that you need to grasp: Just because someone else knows more about the facts does not mean that his information is more pertinent than yours. The crux of your success is what you bring to a particular situation that no one else can. So who's the best candidate for president of the United States? The person who is most expert at running the government? If that were the answer, then career bureaucrats would do well on the campaign trail. No, the best candidate—not necessarily the most qualified person, but the person who is most electable—is whoever comes across with expertise that has the most relevance for the audience in a given context.

Let's take it down another step. Assume that you are trying to explain to a child why a cold glass collects water on the outside. Do you talk about the relative humidity of air and saturation points near the glass, or do you say that cold air makes moisture collect on the outside of the glass? In some cases, simple is good. The audience dictates when simple is unpretentious and when simple is foolish.

In short, you don't have to be the best there is; you have to be right at the moment, matching your information with the audience at hand. A scientist would sound stupid to a child with his description of why the glass "sweats."

Facts and human nature both play into an assessment of both the focus and the role of audience members. I touched on the issue of role in Chapter 2 by examining how and why the natural leader, the genuine expert, and the loud guy would manifest their skepticism, thereby playing roles in your acceptance or rejection as an expert.

Be sure you clarify, as much as possible, what the "why" is. As you assess your audience, spend some time understanding what motivates the individuals who are part of that audience. Can you discover any reasons why someone would be skeptical of you or be predisposed to accept you as an expert? These reasons will affect how you should address the group—whether you should come across as a know-it-all to intimidate people or win the audience over with charm. Maryann and I knew that we would face a mixed audience of skeptics and friendly faces when we gave a presentation at the International Spy Museum, where the regular audience for the lecture series has the opportunity to hear top people from the world of espionage. Our joint presentation reflected that awareness: In classic know-it-all fashion, I controlled the information and pace of the presentation, and Maryann engaged the audience with demonstrations and humanizing stories.

You have to begin this process of uncovering motivation by looking at a few factors that affect a person's drive. Skip this step and you will significantly undermine your information research and planning efforts.

MOTIVATION FACTORS

There are many possibilities for what drives someone toward or away from another person's information. I'm going to take a look at four main ones:

1. Natural inclinations

2. Needs

3. What someone stands to lose

4. What someone stands to gain

NATURAL INCLINATIONS

In addressing the difference between healthy skepticism and a contrarian earlier, I wanted to plant a question in your mind: Is the person you are going to talk to naturally difficult to persuade? If so, you have to get a running start, as you will have an uphill battle. Some people cannot validate you until they understand that you are part of their fan club. If you suspect, or know for sure, that this is the type of person you're dealing with, be prepared to demonstrate your respect for that person before you present any information to convince her that you're an expert. The bottom line is: You can't possibly be smart enough to be an expert unless you are smart enough to appreciate her. I'm not talking about getting out the snorkel here, but simply acknowledging her value prior to your discussion.

There are all sorts of variations on a theme with a person who wants her ego fed. She may be consistently amiable (the politician), or she may snipe because of crippling insecurities (the middle child). Your baselining skills will help you figure out when and if you have won her over. And what if that person who wants an ego stroke is the village idiot? Do you want her on your side? If you win her over and she becomes part of your cheering section, does it do you more harm than good?

Some people are just the opposite: They cannot validate you until you prove your superiority. (Why would a powerful man want a dominatrix?) Again, baselining will give you clues on the spot, but going into the situation, it will help if you have some background on the person's natural inclination.

So take into consideration not only who is in the room and what you know about each person's natural temperament, but also whether you really want and need each person's approval and what you will do with it once you get it. This requires an understanding of each person's place in the hierarchy even more than it requires an understanding of his demeanor and disposition. It also considers what he needs, what he stands to lose, and what he stands to gain.

NEED

When does a person *not* need something—even if it's just someone to listen to her? That condition rarely occurs. If you are in a one-on-one conversation, you should assume that at the very least, the person either wants to connect with someone who understands her point of view or needs the entertainment of a debate partner.

Someone who is new to the company may need validation and a sense of belonging, while the old-timer may need you to remember what he has done for the company. The boss may need a confidant, and anyone else may just need a simple answer to a complex question.

Each person requires a different approach as you attempt to gain acceptance as an expert—a different style of delivery, and a different use of jargon.

A potentially dangerous situation when you're new to a company, whether you're a recent hire or a consultant, is mismatching people's needs with your command of a subject. When you walk into a room and spout enough language and facts about a specialized field to convince a real expert, or at least a devotee, that you can fulfill his need for companionship in a sea of strangers, you may win very quickly. Alternatively, you may lose very quickly. You may get a reply that you are incapable of understanding, and not only alienate the real expert, but also lose the rest of the room.

POTENTIAL LOSS

Change is never easy. When you succeed in coming across to a group as an expert, especially if the people in that group have already known you and have not flagged you as a knowledgeable person, then the group members' status quo changes.

Remember that not accepting you as the expert will enable most people to maintain their status quo. If things are working, why would people want to risk losing status or equity by admitting that you know something they didn't know before your arrival? On the other hand, if things are not working, then there are people in the group who are benefiting from it: Whether they are contrarians or just people who backbite, there are those who are benefiting from every action that turns sour.

Look for who will lose when you establish yourself. Situation 1: You are lucky and no one stands to lose. Situation 2: You see that the leader, the loud guy, or the expert could be rattled by change. Most of us are quite comfortable with existing—even if existing means suffering—in our current state as compared to changing to a new state.

When you approach your audience, start by assuming that change is difficult and most people avoid it. Only when they are properly motivated do most people adopt new ways of thinking, and after all, your being an expert on something they know or need to know is a change. That holds true whether you've just met them or you've known them a long time.

POTENTIAL GAIN

Even when no one obviously stands to benefit from your becoming an expert, your success is likely to create opportunities for others to benefit. Take the example of the office football expert who runs the pool and freely offers advice on winners and losers. Who benefits by your becoming an expert about football? Not the guys who are losing: Now they have an even lower chance of getting a few bucks from the pool. And surely not the reigning expert, because now he has competition.

Focus on what each person stands to gain. You need to package your expertise like a good interrogator. Give the reigning expert someone to talk to on "his level," and interpret what he knows for those who do not know it. That gets you acceptance not only from the reigning expert, but also from the contenders, who consider you to be both an equal to the big guy and a mentor to help them get to the point of being an expert. You win all around because you understood what everyone had to gain.

In order to adequately exploit these tendencies, you will need to take into account the person's motivation as it relates to your desired outcome, and then further understand when duration trumps everything.

THE DESIRED OUTCOME

This factor goes to the heart of why you would want to be an expert in two hours. Is your goal to be adored for your brilliance? To get a job? To seduce someone?

I go into every interrogation with a set of requirements; getting those requirements met is my desired outcome. There's a fluidity to the situation, because as I learn more about my audience—in this case a prisoner or source—the better able I am to refine what it is he can do for me. To some extent, you need to be just as flexible in defining your outcome, because you may walk into a meeting having made a decision about who your audience is, only to discover that she is someone completely different.

Consider all the different steps an interrogator goes through just to identify the desired outcome with certainty—and what a small piece of this process involves acquiring jargon and other new pieces of data.

Professional interrogation is not about theatrics and/or sadists entertaining themselves at the prisoners' expense. The job centers on collecting information, getting as much pertinent information as possible in the least amount of time. So when I prepare for an interrogation, I learn just enough to have sufficient credibility to establish rapport. My aim is to have a strong enough connection to get the person to talk; that allows me to extract information in a timely fashion. That is my desired outcome—nothing more. I have no desire to be perceived as witty, intelligent, kind, or cruel. My desired outcome dictates that I understand enough about my source's life to get him to believe whatever I tell him—lie or truth—

and to extract the information I need without stopping to look up terms and concepts while I question.

My experience has been that interrogators typically conduct sessions for 12 hours at a time, with a debriefing from the previous shift starting an hour before the prescribed start time for the next shift. Add all this up and it really means that interrogators work 14-hour shifts. Generally speaking, the debriefings center on two types of information: an intelligence map, which is all the relevant facts that we have, and a working map, which is what the prisoners are telling us. The intelligence map includes every bit of data we have about the area where the prisoner I'm about to interrogate was captured.

Because of that intelligence map, I may know more about the circumstances of his capture than the prisoner does. If I know enough about his basic job and show some compassion, he will talk to me. He will also identify with me and spill information. In order to make sense of the information he is giving me, though, I need a framework for sorting it. This is the reason for that part of the preparation that equips me with facts, as opposed to insights into the person.

The prisoner may have heard something exploding off in the distance, but I know exactly where the explosion occurred and what it destroyed. So when I ask, "What happened just before you were captured?" and he replies that he heard an explosion over his left shoulder, I can tell exactly where he was standing and which direction he was facing. Similar encounters with other prisoners will tell me where they were in relation to one another, so I can start to put together a three-dimensional picture of the battlefield with these people in it. As I keep building this ostensibly useless information about where people were and what they were doing, I can confirm who was doing what and therefore who might be able to meet my requirements for critical information.

In this process, I usually know a tremendous number of facts that I never divulge to the source. I may know that the unit to his left was utterly destroyed, and when I find out that his brother was in that unit, I may opt to disclose this or not, depending on what I am trying to accomplish. Information is sometimes more powerful when it is not disclosed.

In this situation, I ask myself, "What am I looking for?" Tactical information about the equipment load of that unit? The vulnerabilities of the vehicle he was riding in? How much ammo these vehicles carry? All of these things are part of the basic knowledge of any soldier. Alternatively, I may discover during our conversation that he was the general's driver, rather than an ordinary soldier—a wealth of valuable information. In uncovering that gem, I know that this session will not be the last I will see of him. My expertise will have to sustain me through many more hours of conversation if I am to remain the person I have claimed to be.

THE DURATION OF THE SESSION

Duration is the driving force that helps you know how much information you have to have.

It could be a job interview, a key meeting, or a cocktail party where you want to demonstrate expertise. Each situation puts criteria in play that dictate how long you need to sustain your presentation in order to achieve your desired outcome. If your aim is nothing more than to impress someone in a one-time session that lasts 15 minutes, that's easy. But if you want to sustain the perception of expertise for a long-term outcome, such as a job, then the task at hand is quite different and will involve multiple players in the roles of both skeptic and supporter. So ask yourself:

- How long do I have to sustain expertise in order to succeed?

- When that first meeting is over, will I need to come back and continue presenting this particular expertise, perhaps at a compounded level?

- How much time will I have between sessions?

The information you require is like ammunition at a firefight: You carry too much, and you are weighted down; you carry too little, and you get killed. And when you know a lot about the topic, but not enough about how to use the facts, you are like a gunner without a trigger finger.

To a great extent, your selection of strategy, which I cover in Chapter 5, and the application of methods of demonstrating expertise, such as association and intimidation, rests on how long you have to present your expertise.

Here are the basic considerations:

- You have two hours or less to prepare.

- Expertise of any kind is knowledge intersecting people.

- You have to decide how long your session will be, and the subsets of that are:

  ○ How much time will be dedicated to building rapport, which is obviously dictated by your current relationship? In a short meeting with a new client, a proportionately large amount of time might well be spent on getting to know the person, with the expectation that you come with a degree of familiarity with the topic.

  ○ How long will you have to sustain the show that is your expertise?

Whatever the strategy, you need to remember, just like the soldier, to choose your ammunition carefully. Take into account the person you are talking to, what you intend to accomplish, and how long you have to stay on target. Just as with ammunition, you never want to use everything, even if you think you're done. Keep a few rounds for the inevitable.

5

MODELS OF EXPERTISE—STRATEGY, TECHNIQUES, AND TACTICS

¤ ¤ ¤

In *Rain Man*, Raymond Babbitt (Dustin Hoffman) amazes his brother Charlie (Tom Cruise) by memorizing the alphanumeric designations of all the songs on a tabletop diner jukebox in minutes. Charlie reads the name of the song; Raymond shoots back "G4," "M1," and so on. What's Raymond's strategy for convincing his brother that he's an expert? None. He doesn't even know what an expert is.

A strategy for setting yourself up as an expert means honing your self-awareness, connecting pieces of information in a meaningful way, and matching your presentation style to the situation. Raymond, who is autistic, can't do any of that.

Contrast that with the disarming display of expertise exhibited by actor/politician Fred Thompson, both on the real campaign trail and on TV's *Law & Order*, where he portrays "a hulking prosecutor in chief fond of chastening subordinates with bits of Southern folk wisdom" (*Christian Science Monitor*, May 7, 2007). Like the character Andy Griffith portrayed to teach previous generations that smart doesn't need to be ostentatious, Thompson knows that it isn't facts like Raymond Babbitt's that stick with people—it's having a strategy for making the connection between information and the individual. It's coming across with Forrest Gump–like wisdom, but from the head of someone with a high IQ: just a simple man's understanding of a complex problem.

What you will do in becoming an expert in two hours or less is adopt one or more strategies to present yourself as an expert. Remembering that these strategies are based on a prediction of your audience's motivation, fears, hopes, and needs, as you get to know your audience better, you will then integrate techniques to support your strategy. Finally, your assessment of your audience's responses to you, and how best to get to the desired outcome in the time you have available, will dictate what tactics you use to get there.

Strategies give you ways to manage information.

Techniques help you influence people.

Tactics are ways to display strength.

These factors determine your choice of strategy:

- Your personality
- Your flexibility in the ways you communicate with people
- The amount of time you have to do research
- The amount of time you have to exhibit your expertise
- The type of information you have access to during your preparation
- Audience size
- Audience composition

Since I covered the fundamentals of duration and audience in Chapter 4, I will focus here on personality and information types as a way of moving you into a consideration of strategies.

PERSONALITY

The different ways we've come up with to break down personality types involve information-sorting styles and approaches to interacting with people. Some people cross the threshold to accept someone's expertise because of how data are handled; others do it simply because of how well they relate to the person handling the data.

TECHNICIAN

The technician is a detail-oriented person, one who needs facts. This is my high school geometry teacher: "I do not care about the answer, Mr. Hartley. I want to see how you get from point A to point B. Getting the answer right does not mean you understand the process." Precision with facts means a great deal to the technician, and not having it causes stress. If you are such a person, you place great emphasis on the source of information, and you could end up being your own biggest skeptic in trying to present expertise. If a person of this type is in your audience, one of his requirements for accepting you as the expert is going to be detail.

GENERALIST

People with this personality type absorb information about lots of subjects and show agility in quickly grasping correlations. I remember a TV commercial in which a little girl said something like, "I want to grow up to be a scientist. My daddy's a scientist." And then to somebody else, "I want to grow up to be a weatherman. My daddy's a weatherman." And then to somebody else, "I want to grow up to be a veterinarian. . . ." Finally, someone who'd heard her answers gave her a hard time. "You told us your daddy is a . . ." And she just said, "Yeah. My daddy's a farmer." In modern society, the professional who may come closest to being the kind of expert that thrived in primitive societies is the farmer. He's a generalist: a good example of someone who can adapt and succeed with no specialization. The generalist understands things in terms of how they relate to one another better than she understands vast amounts of details about a specific area. If you are a generalist, you have a natural edge as an expert. You just need to remember when you are preparing that the technicians in your audience need details, because not having enough facts will cost you credibility with them. If you are not a generalist, you may find this type of person's need to understand how all of your details tie into the big picture a bit frustrating. Remember that all of your details mean nothing to the generalist unless you can translate them into meaning.

STORYTELLER

It seems like everything reminds this type of person of "the time when . . . ," and she is naturally entertaining in using bits from her life, TV, movies, and other people's lives to highlight points. This can drive a detail person crazy, as she tells him stories when all he wants are facts. Understanding how to weave good stories like fables, the storyteller can create a bridge between the generalist and the technician without ever becoming either of them. The storyteller needs to tell stories that have a message that addresses questions squarely, allays concerns, and reminds the listener what is in it for him.

SPONGE

Strongly affected by other people's opinions and gullible about information, the sponge will easily accept someone's expertise because of that person's affiliation, among other reasons. You're a doctor; therefore you must know what you're talking about. These people created the market for TV shows like *Myth Busters* and web sites like urbanlegends.com. They are continually looking for a simple answer to a complex problem, and when they hear one, they absorb it, details and all. Like a sponge, when they are squeezed for information, they release what they have heard. If you are like this, you need to pay close attention to the section in Chapter 6 on vetting your source. When you are dealing with people like this, you may create a tense situation when you challenge something that they believe to be true. And the facts may have little to do with their truth.

ROMANTIC

Just like the basic definition, these are fanciful adventure seekers who are idealistic. Being affected more by the meaning of information than by the facts, romantics are prone to disregard the facts in favor of feelings. When they do find facts to support their fancies, watch out. No one has more passion. Arguing with an on-cause romantic is tilting at windmills. These are people who look for meaning where there may be little. If you are on the same wavelength and support their ideas, they reciprocate with full support. If you fall short of their *ideal*, however, you may have a hard battle ahead. If you are a romantic, learn to home in on practical information in your research. Do not follow the rabbit down the hole to find out if there is a Wonderland. By this I mean that when you see something that supports your belief, look past it to get more facts. Other people will require those facts. If you are dealing with a romantic, try not to rain on his parade; instead, show him how to use the information you are offering to feed his picture of the world.

BLENDED STYLES

The personality types just discussed are categorization tools, and, like all such descriptions of human beings, they shouldn't be considered rigid definitions. Many (most) people will be combinations of these styles. Think of yourself, for instance. Are you an idealist? Maybe you're a romantic who is also a sponge, constantly looking for the latest data to support your worldviews and ready to repeat this information on a moment's notice. Or maybe you're a generalist who is also a romantic, constantly wondering how things connect in the overall scheme of things. People are complex and blended. I can represent anyone somewhere on a bell curve for each of these attributes. Your job is to take into account how your *audience* thinks, as well as how you think, to understand how best to present your case.

INFORMATION TYPES

Depending upon your source, the information you collect can be descriptive, anecdotal, statistical, or opinionated. "Just the facts" will not satisfy everyone. If that were all people wanted, then we could just connect to the Internet and forget about listening to one another. For many people, anecdotes are enough; for others, you need more concrete clinical evidence supported by studies. Still others trust the numbers or statistics more. Since humans are archetypal thinkers, anchoring our thoughts around concepts, you can prey on that by bringing stories and universally accepted truths to the fore in relation to your information. By understanding your audience and how you can best compartmentalize information for that audience, you can design a set of tools to deliver your own version of expertise. You could spend a month collecting data off the Internet about which toothpaste is best for you; you might know everything there is to know about the subject, but how you present that information determines whether or not anyone will listen to you.

With data all over the map, from precise facts to outlandish conspiracy theory, how much validity any of it holds for you, as well as for members of your audience, may well depend on your and their personality type. For example, a technician who is trying to become an expert in two hours will go straight for the facts. If he wants to be able to discuss the 1968 Tet Offensive during the Vietnam War, he will find out how historians describe it rather than call his friend's dad who served in Vietnam and probably knows someone who told him stories about what might have happened. A storyteller might go to www.imdb.com and find a movie about Vietnam, or talk to that father of a friend or even the friend's mother to better understand the human impact of the war.

Is one method better than the other? The answer depends partially on what you connect with best, but it also depends on who your audience is and how facile you are with a particular kind of information. If you are a sponge, for example, you may have a difficult time hunting down statistics and highlighting them in a presentation, especially if your audience is made up of technicians.

For most types of people, statistics are the least desirable type of information for proving expertise. They can serve you well when you're on the offensive, trying to determine whether or not someone is being honest with you, but they can easily trip you up if you use them as a cornerstone of your expertise.

Here's an example of how you can use them in an offensive way: Someone says, "Half of America's kids are overweight." You happen to have read that the latest study indicates that it's about 25 percent, so you say simply, "They're probably overweight by someone's terms, but I've read that doctors would call only 25 percent of them fat." But does this challenge set you up as an expert, or just a contrarian?

Now consider another way this might play out. "Half of all kids are overweight!" And you respond, "Really? Does that take into account the weight that many children gain prior to puberty that is quickly lost as part of the puberty growth spurt?" You have not actually relied on facts, and so you do not need to quote a statistic to question the credibility of the statement and the speaker. You have preyed on people's memory of their own life or the lives of others. Alternatively, you could say, "How do you define overweight? Whose scale? What percentage of body fat?" In that case, you could hold on to your information that doctors say that a quarter of the nation's children have xx percent or more body fat as your final weapon.

Misuse of statistics not only undermines your credibility, but makes you look like a fool. Do you want to sound like Alfalfa in *The Little Rascals*? Discovering in a book that "every fifth born child is Chinese," he decided that it was a scary thing that his mother was expecting another child—her fifth. This interpretation of facts without context is common.

This is one example of why statistics are not knowledge; by themselves, they convey no expertise. Nevertheless, if you're a technician who wants to train yourself to be more discerning about using them, go to www.econoclass.com and take the test on misleading statistics that's designed for high school and college economics students. For example, what would your response be to this statement: The best public schools offer a more challenging curriculum than most private schools. If you said, public schools are obviously better than private schools, then you fell into the trap. All this statement does is compare the best of one to most of another. That makes no sense.

Now that I have discouraged you from using statistics, I will admit that, in the hands of someone who understands human nature, statistics can be a powerful tool. Given the right audience—say, an audience of sponges—you could get away with the bogus public-versus-private school statistic and get people into a full-blown debate about the state of education. As long as you can walk away from the discussion before you have to say anything else, you may even look smart.

As you move into strategies, you need to consider what you are trying to achieve, what motivates your audience, and how its members deal with information as well as how long you have to maintain your role as expert. This is, of course, influenced by your information management style and how well you can adapt.

STRATEGIES

Strategies capture a way of managing information so that you exhibit expertise. They are ways of showing what you know and avoiding what you don't know. As I mentioned, not every strategy is a good match for every person, nor is a strategy that you feel comfortable with going to work with every audience. In fact, some of these strategies can't even be done if your audience is a single person.

SPIDER

The Spider's web is interconnected ideas, and the Spider's skill is moving from one idea to another one that she knows more about—

and then to yet another that she knows even more about. It's being adept at working with everything you have.

Here's an example of people who failed miserably at doing this in a physical sense; it's a good metaphor for pointing out the way this strategy works, or doesn't.

I have a friend who runs an adventure training camp where people pay to learn about the prisoner-of-war experience. The focus in one particular exercise was to go through what average prisoners of war in Third World countries were treated like, without the torture. I threw down a bunch of brittle sticks and said, "If you can make a sleeping mat—each—no, wait; if the ten of you can make just one sleeping mat in two hours with these sticks, you can have eight hours sleep."

These guys were tired and miserable; the prospect of sleep seemed like heaven to them. They had hardly anything more than rain ponchos and these sticks.

In two hours, I came back and they had a tiny square—it could be measured in inches—that they had woven out of the sticks. Dismayed by their lack of progress, I pulled a few slim strips from one guy's poncho, wove it between the sticks, and made a six-foot long sleeping mat in five minutes.

Again, you have to work with everything you have, and they obviously did not.

I continued the conversation with this group, made up of a lot of very successful corporate folks. I gave them exercises similar to the sleeping mat challenge, and they were not getting it. Finally, I asked them what separates humans from most animals. One guy yelled, "Thumbs." "I hate to break this to you," I said, "but monkeys have thumbs." We kept on this track, and they came up with answers like "communication." "All animals communicate," I told them. Finally, one guy got it: "Adaptability."

Animals can adapt to different environments, but not to every environment. Humans claim the prize in being able to adapt to a wide variety of environments. We have the gift of being able to generalize, to make correlations.

Then I took them down the rabbit hole. I told them that my ability to make a sleeping mat displayed that human ability, but that they must be more like animals, since they failed. I said, "In fact, you've become so specialized—you banker, you cinematographer, you lawyer, you professor—that you are subhuman."

All I had asked them to do was look internally at what they knew and make correlations with the external environment. You can call it nothing more than common sense, if you like, but this catch-all concept is fundamental to using the Spider strategy to succeed as an expert. It is using the white matter that you have to make the connections that the Rain Man cannot. In working with a filmmaker named Adam Larsen on a documentary about the autistic recently, I learned a lot about the condition that is relevant here. High-functioning autistics do make connections and, in fact, can do some of the very exercises that I gave the executives in ways that the executives could not because of their *specialization*. This should drive home the point that humans can be represented on a bell curve for all things. Keep this in mind as you apply these skills.

I once visited an old friend's grandmother in a nursing home. She and others in the ward suffered from advanced cases of Alzheimer's disease. One little woman spoke so brilliantly at times that I kept forgetting that her wheels turned differently from mine. She had been a professor at Vanderbilt University, and that career defined her. Whenever she drifted into her alternative reality, everything circled back to Vanderbilt. After a while, I forgot that she had Alzheimer's disease because she was so charming and articulate. I realized that my friend had gone out of the room, and I asked her, "Did you see where that tall, blonde woman went?" "Yes," she said. "If you go right out that door there and take a left, you'll be at Vanderbilt. She's at Vanderbilt."

Although she wasn't doing it intentionally, she was doing the Spider. Everything related back to a point of reference that she understood.

The Spider requires the ability to move a conversation laterally, so that you get to subjects, or aspects of the subject, about which you know something. As a corollary, you keep the discussion away from areas that you don't know anything about.

Try the following exercise as a way to warm up.

Be cautious and intelligent in your approach to how you do this, or you will end up looking stupid. My particular brand of knowledge—human behavior—lends itself to the Spider very well. Your specialty in operating room technology may not.

STONE SOUP

In the fable about stone soup, a stranger comes into a town that's suffering from famine. No one offers him anything to eat because they have so little. He parks himself in the middle of town, builds a fire, pulls out a big iron pot, fills it with water, and places it on top of the fire. Then he takes a clean stone out of a beautiful silk bag and drops it in the water. He soon dips a ladle into the water and sips the stone soup. "Mmmm," he says. "Delicious! But I've had it made with cabbage, and it is extraordinary." So one of the villagers brings out a tiny cabbage that he's been hoarding and drops it in the pot. The stranger's "mmms" continue until the pot has salt pork, carrots, potatoes, and onions. He then shares the stone soup with everyone, and the villagers marvel at how wonderful it is and offer to buy the stranger's "magic stone."

When you use this strategy, you're the recipe holder, not the cook. You come into the room with the expertise of listening and making correlations between the pieces of information that other people are offering. Your job as an expert is to make those people feel confident enough to contribute to the soup. This is coalition

EXERCISE: THE KEVIN BACON GAME

Remember the six-degrees-of-separation game, aka the Kevin Bacon game? The mathematical premise is that everybody on earth is, by association, only six people away from everyone else. The illustration, if you will, is that every movie actor has only six degrees of separation from Kevin Bacon. In this exercise, you do it with information. Pick two topics that seem to be widely separated. Here are a few suggestions:

GENOCIDE IN RWANDA . . . . .401(K) PLANS

CANADIAN THISTLES. . . . . PARIS HILTON

MUDSLIDES .MICROSOFT CORPORATION

Here is a light hearted example of how the exercise might work:

1. A homeowner in the San Francisco Bay Area talks about the disturbing possibility that her house could go into the ocean if there were heavy storms in her area.

2. You ask what precautions she's taken.

3. The homeowner talks about insurance, reverse 911, keeping a lot of emergency supplies in the car, and so on.

4. You say, "You seem more prepared than most corporations. You've thought of all the contingencies! I bet if you worked for Microsoft, my computer would never crash!"

Okay, I did it in four steps. How about you?

building of the highest order because it uses the motivation of the participants. Everyone remembers his own contribution, but you are at the center of the event.

REFINER

I call this strategy the Refiner because in a room with experts, the information coming from them is so often like crude oil—useless. Crude oil is a mixture of hundreds of different types of hydrocarbons that have to be separated in order to provide gas for your car, lubricating oil, kerosene, and then, further down the line, things like plastics and crayons. It's the fractional distillation process used in refineries that gives crude oil its value.

Our culture is about the end use of products, not raw goods like crude oil. What does an American who's just leaving a diner say when you ask, "What did you just have for breakfast?" A common response might be "A Swiss cheese omelet, bacon, wheat toast, and home fries." The person might also assume that you're asking because you want to know the quality of the breakfast so that you can decide whether or not to eat at that diner, so the omelet might be "delicious" or "runny." In many other parts of the world, however, you might hear nothing more than "Eggs, meat, bread, and potatoes" because people think more in terms of raw goods. This mentality affects the way we want information presented to us. Don't make us work too hard to see the value. Prepare the information for consumption and then put it in neat plastic baggies that stack well on the shelves in our mind.

The Refiner is especially useful in the face of overwhelming amounts of information that no one can use. In July 2002, shortly after World Wide Web co-inventor Sir Tim Berners-Lee first began publishing papers about the new "semantic Web," he gave a presentation about it in Boston. The people in attendance rushed out of the conference room saying, "What did he say? What does it mean? Who can explain this?" In short, they were looking for a Refiner, someone who could glean the facts and present them in a usable form. A good Refiner uses broad, general explanations, often in parable form, that allow each user to understand the information on his own level. The refiner simply breaks this very technical information into large chunks that have meaning to all people on an archetypal level and allows each person to fill in the meaning for her daily life. In this way a Refiner may contribute understanding that even he himself does not have.

INTERPRETER

A genuine subject-matter expert can keep a sense of awe going in a presentation or conversation, and thereby set herself up as someone who can't be challenged. As an Interpreter, you play off of the expert to bring home to the audience members what part of the information connects to their world and their point of view. You understand the audience. You know its members' level of understanding, and you become the cog that makes the machine work. Religious experts have done this for millennia when interpreting the will of god into human terms. Your expertise is that you are the one who can interpret the expert to others. You don't want to be the Oracle at Delphi; you want to be the temple priest. This differs from the Refiner because you are translating specific ideas and language into language for common use.

If you can understand the subject-matter expert's language, then you are valuable, but you have to be deferential enough not to threaten him. If he thinks that you aren't just interpreting for him, but really understand his secrets, then you become dangerous. You don't want that person to lose credibility, because then you will be under attack.

The Interpreter can be part of a sophisticated strategy. If you go into a room where you know nothing, there may be lots of people who are highly specialized, but who don't speak the same language. Take a marketing guy and a software guy. You can come across as an expert, and seem brilliant in the process, if you can interpret what each is saying to the other in simplistic terms. You become the most important person at the meeting because you help people make sense to each other; you establish the language bridges that enable ideas to move smoothly.

In the first Gulf War, I was traveling with the Kuwaiti Army. There were three Americans and ten Kuwaitis sitting in a tent near a power station that was smoldering because the Iraqis had thrown hand grenades into the transformers when they pulled out.

It was my job to work out the terms for clearing an area called Hawalee. Sitting in this tent, we negotiated with the Kuwaitis what we wanted them to say in their native language for our Psychological Ops guys to play on the speaker system. We chose to broadcast in their dialect rather than using my Arabic, which is more formal than theirs. On the tape, which would loop over and over, we wanted them to say something like, "Turn in your weapons. Do not fire on us. We are here to liberate the city. We are here to find Iraqis. If you know where they are, come tell us." We also wanted to make it clear that, "If you shoot at us, then we will retaliate."

What they had in mind was more like, "All criminals come out now or we will level the buildings."

In the course of the negotiation, as I translated what the Kuwaiti colonel said for one of our officers, our guy didn't like the way things were going and said, "You tell that so-of-a-**** that . . ." At that point, I became more than an interpreter; I became an advisor by conveying the relevant piece of information, but not the insult.

I may not have been the smartest guy or the best interpreter, but at that moment, I was exactly what everyone needed to get the job done. I was the expert who could get things to work.

INTERROGATOR

This strategy centers on solving a problem, rather than on the sheer demonstration of expertise. The Interrogator extracts information for information's sake, then, upon determining the data the rest of the group requires to get the job done, reaching for those data and bringing them to the forefront. The Interrogator is nonjudgmental, not commenting on the quality of the information he receives, but simply extracting as much relevant information as possible to address the problem at hand.

You learn to do this in two hours or less by focusing on skills such as following *source leads*, or forks in the conversation that the person presents. When people talk or even ask questions, they are constantly divulging information. Think of a conversation at a party and how it flows, constantly taking turns based on what is said—now you understand what a source lead is. In short, you take collection requirements from the cues of those around you and build an effective questioning plan by using data you know from research. Quite simply, this is being the voice of everyone's unspoken questions, which in some cases they could not frame.

PEARL

The Pearl is the most sophisticated strategy and takes the most talent. The concept is that a little piece of knowledge is like the sand in the oyster. By using source leads to drive the conversation, you put layer upon layer of discussion on top of that grain of sand, so that you consistently build on top of it. By the end of the conversation—and this is more likely to be a session that lasts hours than one of short duration—the other person (or people) does not even have a clue that you started the conversation relatively ignorant. It's because of how you released the information and built one thing on top of another.

The best journalists are adept at this method of establishing expertise, but you rarely see the process in action unless you catch them in a multipart documentary. The snippets you get on the evening news deliver the result without showing the hours of interaction that went into creating it.

During our discussions about this strategy, Maryann recalled that she may have inadvertently done this a number of times in researching her first book, which was about telemedicine. In it, she relied heavily on building a rapport with an unusual breed of doctor in 1993: one who had nearly as much technological expertise as he did medical knowledge. Here, in roughly recreated dialogue, is a conversation with an Army physician that illustrates the use of the Pearl:

Maryann:	"Your telemedicine operation in Somalia set precedents."
Dr. G.:	"Yes, it did."
Maryann:	"Using the PowerBook as the centerpiece technology made it so portable."
Dr. G.:	"It was so easy to plug in the camera and interface with the satellite. The whole package weighed less than 30 pounds."
Maryann:	"Was weight an issue in bringing this kind of thing into the evac hospital?"
Dr. G.:	"Yes, but we also had power issues. That computer had the ability to go from electricity to battery without a hitch. In a power outage, you knew it would switch from one mode to the other without loss of data."
Maryann:	"Other computers didn't do that?"
Dr. G.:	"No. We researched all the components of the system carefully so that we had a system that was as durable as possible, but also as flexible as possible in terms of power issues, storage, and so on."
Maryann:	"I know the continued use of this prototype means that you have some great success stories."

Dr. G. then told a number of success stories, which inherently contained explanations about the use of the technology, diagnostic procedures, treatment protocols, financial aspects of the project, and much more. Was Maryann perceived as an expert by the end of it? The interview led to more than just a chapter in the book; it led to a consulting position drafting and editing telemedicine-related journal articles and other materials for Walter Reed Army Medical Center.

What was the "grain of sand"? The knowledge that the Power-Book was the core technology in the scheme. Everything else was a compliment or a leading question, that is, something to use to pursue a source lead.

One final note on this. There's an old Army adage, "No plan ever survives the first contact with the enemy." Your strategy may change, therefore, once you are at the scene. The better you know

EXERCISE: UNDERSTANDING INADVERTENT SUCCESS

Think of a time, whether it was last week at work or years ago in high school, when someone you thought was "an idiot" emerged as an expert. What did this person do that immediately got people to pay attention to him and show him some respect? Can you match that accomplishment with any of the strategies listed earlier?

The names of the strategies are not important; you may come up with a list of your own that provides better anchors for you. The important thing is that you have a strategy, as your strategy will help you narrow down how you are going to do research. If you don't know how you are going to approach the person or the group, then you don't know how to do research.

your audience in advance, the less likely it is that you will have to make dramatic changes.

INEPT VERSUS ADEPT

Deliberate use of the strategies discussed here will keep you mindful of the mechanics of the situation, and of ways to prevent the kind of failures I describe here. In these scenarios, the "experts" fell into patterns without realizing their potential. All you have to do is listen with the six strategies in mind and you will hear the sound of near misses, just as these people try to present themselves as experts.

I either participated personally in the situations I'm about to describe or learned about them from people I know well. I have made small changes in the descriptions to protect the inept.

SPIDER

The CEO of a small company was hosting a business dinner in honor of a client. Two members of his staff were also at the table, and one of them was a new hire who seemed desperate to please. The client talked about a pet project of hers: researching and writing a magazine article about hate literature. The CEO asked if she had a main source she was using to define the concept, and she replied, "Yes. The Southern Poverty Law Center."

Before anyone could take another breath, the new hire jumped into the conversation with facts and anecdotes about the terrible situation involving the Jena 6, the black teenagers who took civil rights into their own hands in Jena, Louisiana. People at the table listened politely as the input, which showed a great deal of knowledge, derailed the discussion.

Problem: The new hire had made the connection in his head between the Southern Poverty Law Center and the news item, but never expressed it. As a result, the topic seemed like a non sequitur.

How he should have used the strategy: The president of the Center had written about the Jena 6 situation, so the connection between the topic on the table and the "area of expertise" of the new hire was actually a tight one. He could have introduced that fact, offered a few impressive facts, and then easily looped back to the client by asking if her research covered anything related to the Jena 6. Remember that a Spider navigates her web by moving systematically from her current location to the location of her prey, not by simply hopping over the web to the new location. Think of the conversation as being a flowing, living thing, and navigate the conversation through ancillary prompts that drive the conversation back to your area of knowledge.

STONE SOUP

The owner of a midsized PR agency hired a senior person for project management and, as her first assignment, told the new person to coordinate a campaign for a barter exchange. The owner gave the new person no preparation time; he said, "Your team's in there waiting for you," and opened the meeting room door. Looking around the room at the eager junior executives, who had notes in front of them, she hoped that at least they knew something about the company. She began by saying that she was looking forward to illustrating the "modern face" of bartering and invited thoughts. One person noted that the company founders were handsome, young entrepreneurs, so promoting them would help. Another said that success stories involving some of their exchange members, like technology companies, top hotels, and others with a modern face, would get the job done. A third suggested that the PR agency join the exchange and do a story about how it had personally experienced the benefits of bartering. The new project manager knew that the owner would never allocate agency resources for anything but real money, but she went ahead and added it to the draft plan.

Problem: The project manager realized that this junior member had just poured vinegar into her soup, but she didn't know how to undo the damage.

How she should have used the strategy: Welcome the idea of following the experiences of a company from the moment it joins the exchange, but blow past the suggestion that the agency itself do it. When Stone Soup does not immediately succeed, the expert needs to become an arbitrator of ideas, adjusting the mix to get the desired outcome. The person making stone soup is the recipe owner and does not allow someone to put spoiled or inappropriate ingredients into it.

REFINER

A consortium made up of a number of research and manufacturing firms wanted to promote the benefits of RFID (radio-frequency identification) technology, so it called a press conference. A handful of reporters came, mostly for the sandwiches, and were stupefied by the facts presented by the technicianlike delivery of the engineers. The meeting organizer tried to explain that this was useful stuff—in transportation, education, retail, in fact, just about everywhere. However, putting this capability into products, animals, and even people to track their moves sounded intrusive. The reporters concluded that RFID technology sounded way too much like part of an Orwellian Big Brother plot.

Problem: The Refiner distilled the information to the point where people heard only the intrusive aspects of the technology. By taking people so far into specific applications that he thought were trendy, he missed the grander opportunity to help them see how the technology can help humanity identify the origins of food, ensure the safety of pets, track property, and so on. He engendered only negative images of how the "mad scientists" would use the technology instead of allowing his audience to fill in the ways in which this would help them.

How he should have used the strategy: If he had provided examples of how RFID is used in transportation (transponders on tollways), education (replacing barcodes on library books), and retail (supply-chain management), the technology suddenly would have come across not only as a time saver, but also as something practical and harmless. Showing how people can protect their pets, protect the world's food supply, and even ensure the proper dispensing of medication takes the use of the technology to the next step while allowing each person to imagine new positive applications that he otherwise might never have even thought of.

PEARL

This conversation illustrates both success and stumbling with the Pearl. One of my friends likes listening to audiobooks instead of paying attention to the road while she's driving; she had just finished one of the CDs of *Don't Know Much About the Universe*, by Kenneth C. Davis. (It took a lot less than two hours, by the way.) So at a party, she decided to come across as an expert on astronomy. She knew that people at the gathering would be smart and well educated, but she had no idea whether or not any of them had any background in the subject.

First, she had to move the conversation toward astronomy. The routes to any particular topic are endless. We steer conversations all the time if we have a funny story to tell or if we want to name drop. Usually, it's a not-so-subtle, "That reminds me of . . ." In this case, the route could have been anything from an obvious reference to a shuttle landing to a meandering from a discussion of religion in America. (Protestant roots in the Reformation; begun by Martin Luther, contemporary of another man who bucked the Catholic Church, the astronomer Copernicus . . .) At this gathering, the people around my friend began talking about plastic surgery. After admitting that she had had a nose job, my friend segued to the oddest nose job of all time: Tycho Brahe replacing a piece of his nose—lost in a duel—with a bridge of silver and gold. After that, the conversation went something like this:

Barry: Who's that?

David: He was the one who proved that Copernicus was right.

Melissa: Yeah. In between parties, he built instruments to observe the stars and planets.

David: I mostly think of him as a mathematician—I think I first heard about him in a college math class—but he is a lot better known for how he applied the math to astronomy.

Barry: When was this?

Melissa: He lived around the same time as Shakespeare.

David: Oh, I remember now. Johannes Kepler was his heir-apparent, and that was so weird because Kepler was completely strait-laced and Tycho Brahe basically got kicked out of one place after another.

Melissa: One of the oddest partnerships ever.

As David continued to recall Tycho's extraordinary accomplishments, Melissa did nothing more than punctuate them with comments about his colorful character—because that was the main thing she had taken away from listening to the CD. Yet, as the conversation drifted in another direction, David commented: "I had no idea you were such a student of astronomy!"

Feeling victorious in her little game, she then went a little bit too far. For starters, she did not keep in mind that, if you only have 30 minutes worth of material and you talk for 32, something you say will sound like gibberish. Someone asked her a seemingly basic question when she took a breath: "Kepler's a much bigger name. Did he actually get credit for the stuff that Brahe did?" Awkward silence. Her credibility slipped backwards a bit.

Problem: As I mentioned in the introduction to the discussion of strategies, the Pearl is the most sophisticated. The challenge is to keep the conversation on track, nurturing the buildup of information. In this case, by blathering on, she could no longer orchestrate the accumulation of complementary facts.

How she should have used the strategy: She should have stopped when she had clearly gained acceptance, and then changed the subject. She could then use the data she had collected in this exchange to educate her research for the next encounter. The sheer volume of information she could amass in another two-hour session would add enough expertise to ensure that David would continue thinking of her as a fellow astronomy aficionado.

INTERPRETER

Failing in this strategy is probably the most laughable. One way for the Interpreter to fall on his face is to finish the sentence of the subject-matter expert. Upon hearing, "The fractional distillation process begins with heating the mixture—," he jumps in with, "and ends with things like crayons and plastic bottles." One of my former Army buddies saw this setup for failure time after time with one of the men he worked with in Washington, DC. After his retirement, this guy, a highly decorated military man, got the top post at a trade association, where he was expected to be conversant in various issues related to the electronics industry and its legislative agendas. Members of his staff would diligently prepare slide presentations for the board of directors to update them on the activities of the group. Wanting to show that he was in charge, he routinely "interpreted" the slides of his staff while they were delivering their presentations, a move that invariably led the presentations in an unintended direction.

Problem: Interpreting is supposed to clarify concepts and nomenclature, and to stick precisely to the point; otherwise it's nothing more than an intrusion that makes the interpreter look like a fool.

How he should have used the strategy: The fundamental rule of using this strategy is understanding the language of both parties. There is no need for deep understanding; rather, what is needed is a good enough grasp to be the best in the room. All this executive needed to do was call his senior staff together in advance of the meeting and have them explain their slides to him "as if they were talking to someone who knew nothing."

In some cases, the best interpreter is the guy who has exactly enough information reinforced by the backbone to take a chance. I was a good linguist, but not the best I knew in my Army unit. I stood out, though, because few of the others were gutsy enough to talk when they were uncertain. Balance is everything.

During Operation Desert Storm, we needed tools. My high-minded Arabic training in politics, science, and military matters had neglected things like pliers and pipe wrenches. I was not intimidated and did not mind looking stupid, so I asked someone we were working with, "Do you have some of that stuff you put on electric wires when you connect them to protect yourself from electricity?" The young Arab looked quizzically at me as he said in Arabic, "Do you mean 'tape'?" Other linguists around me felt too stupid to say that very thing—but I got the tape. So in that case, it made me a better interpreter than the better linguist.

INTERROGATOR

As for real interrogators, the biggest danger with this strategy is projecting what the outcome should be and leading the source to that outcome. The Interrogator needs to keep an open mind and let the subject-matter expert answer the questions as he extracts the information in a systematic way to get resolution.

The Interrogator strategy is aimed at solving a specific problem, so the most inept displays of it result in making the problem worse. There must be a million examples of consultants doing exactly that and tearing down entire companies. This example wasn't quite so catastrophic.

At a communications strategy session with the CEO and four senior company executives, the communications consultant led the executives in a brainstorming session about renaming a product line. She had some very clever ideas, and she was pleased to find that, as she continued the session, the answers to the questions she posed seemed to point right back to her clever ideas. She made checklists and charts, putting up a list of pros versus cons that summarized the issues related to all of the ideas. Ultimately, the group chose her top pick—which the sales team completely rejected the following week.

Problem: In using the Interrogator strategy, the expert cannot impose her agenda on the problem-solving exercise. She has to build collection requirements from the sources at hand—and that means including all relevant sources, not just the ones that agree with her.

How she should have used the strategy: Expanding the vision of options for success would necessitate getting input from people on the front line, many of whom are technicians, in addition to the generalists at the top of the corporate ladder.

TECHNIQUES

In military parlance, the techniques used to get people to talk during an interrogation are called *approaches.* They are ways of handling information and affecting the way people feel about you—psychological levers, if you will. Your choice of techniques depends on how your audience is responding to your strategy and what needs to happen next in order for the audience members to accept you as an expert.

In Chapter 1, I addressed reasons why people would be inclined to accept you as an expert—you're affiliated with people they respect, you intimidate them, and so on. The techniques covered here are the mechanics behind those reasons. You use them to associate, intimidate, affiliate, and so on.

Prime techniques are:

- **Direct questioning.** You can use direct questioning as a way of building on information you have and clarifying things you don't understand. You will sound more intelligent, and suggest that you have confidence in the facts you've already put out there, if you ask for an explanation or definition rather than misuse a concept or term.

Direct questioning works with any strategy.

- **Offering incentives.** Think "campaign promises." People will be quite inclined to view you as an expert if you offer them something they want, whether it's a tangible item or a bit of information that will make their life easier. Think back to the discussion about motivation. An incentive can be as simple as reassuring the person who has a lot to lose that he is safe.

  Incentives can work with any strategy.

- **Playing on emotions.** When strong emotions come into play, then logic takes a back seat. So going back to the example of the bogus statistic on public versus private schools, if you position your statement in such a way that you push hot buttons for the people listening to you, then that statement may not come under as much scrutiny. You run the risk, of course, of alienating people whose negative emotions were aroused by your statement. You might convince a technophobic listener that RFID is a good thing, for example, by pointing out how many dogs are euthanized daily because the owner cannot be found, but that this tragedy could often be averted by using the technology to identify an animal's owner.

  This technique would not work particularly well with a Refiner or Interpreter strategy, where your role is dealing cleanly with information.

- **Criticism.** This can be a mechanism of intimidation, but it can also serve you well with a strategy like Stone Soup. A challenge like "Why do you think that migrating to open-source software won't work?" could be the critical question that gets ideas about a solution flowing into the pot. Intelligent criticism of an argument can also show respect for a person— some people think you "just don't get it" unless you engage them in debate; they are more inclined to accept you as an expert if you argue with them. (Think New Yorkers.)

Criticism would not work well with the Interpreter strategy, but it could be useful with every other strategy. You have to know your audience very well, though.

- **Flattery.** This is grease to keep the conversation moving. In interrogator-speak, we call this pride-and-ego up. The more intelligent your audience is, the more subtle you need to be.

  As long as you sound sincere, you can use this anytime to get people on your side.

- **Futility.** Have you ever been around a little kid who constantly asks, "Why?" When someone starts to spit explanations designed to undermine your credibility, you want to be that little kid. You want to be sure that this person's attempt to take people down his rabbit hole is futile, and one way to do this is by asking for more and more explanation of the points he makes. It's a sure way to make even a wise man sound like a fool.

  This is not a good fit with a Spider or Interpreter strategy.

- **Omniscience.** In Army jargon, that's "we know all." Your body language and judicious use of facts can make you come across like Wikipedia. Ironically, this is a technique that is better utilized by people who know when to shut up than by people who are good talkers. You release key pieces of information at critical junctures in the conversation. This works best when you offer tidbits that no one expected you to have in your head. In an interrogation setting, it usually involves my knowledge of personal facts about the prisoner, or even things such as the source of an explosion he heard right before his capture. In business, I may drop a critical piece of jargon that only the initiates of that specialty are supposed to understand; this would support my Interpreter strategy.

You can support any strategy with this.

- **Ignorance, or naïveté.** Just as there are times when you want to project the idea that you know it all, there are times that it will serve you well to say, "I don't know" or "I'm just like a hog with a wristwatch." This can give you a perfect setup for pulling more information out of people who are more knowledgeable than you are. Even when this ploy yields nothing more, you still inflate your credibility as an honest person—that is, someone who is honest about what she knows and doesn't know—when you invite people to teach you. You learn what you need to learn to feed your own expertise, and you move up a notch, both with the person who answers you and with others in the room. I'm a southerner so I can say this: Southerners do this exceedingly well, à la Georgia Tech grad Jeff Foxworthy and "you might be a redneck" jokes.

  This works especially well with the Pearl and the Interrogator.

- **Establishing common ground.** Think back to the principle of the Kevin Bacon Game and six degrees of separation. You can attract answers and acceptance if you can establish a common affiliation like a college fraternity, Rotary, a women's organization, a charity, the Boy Scouts, or even having fathers who died of the same disease. Common ground gets easier to find with age because we start to notice our eyesight diminishing and our hairline, waistline, or facial lines changing. That's automatic common ground.

It never hurts to make a personal connection with your audience. This works with any strategy and is invaluable in building rapport.

- **Silence.** Golden? Absolutely. Most people, especially in an American culture, cannot tolerate silences, and so they break them with words. They could be rambling, or they could have pearls of wisdom. Listen, and then jump back into the conversation when you have something powerful to say that confirms your expertise.
Silence supports any strategy.

I want you to go back to the point in Chapter 1 that the ways in which you can set yourself up as an expert fall into passive and active categories. These techniques might highlight one of the passive ways—isolation and affiliation—but they also serve as mechanisms for actively achieving demonstration, association, generalization, humanization, adaptation, and intimidation.

TACTICS

Tactics are ploys that support your strategy by providing you with a way to display your strength. They help you to overpower the "enemy," or, in the vernacular of business, they help you to close the deal—to gain acceptance as an expert and either move on, having accomplished your outcome, or go to the next level (and meeting) with your audience.

The most succinct way to describe them is through standard military terms:

- **Barraging**. In a business context, inundating your target with fire means using facts in rapid succession to show a compelling strength. For example, you might use the Spider to loop the conversation back to a subject about which you know a great deal and stay on it by using data, stories, practical insights, and so on to reinforce acceptance of your expertise.

- **Sniper fire.** A sniper fires cautiously on a specific target in a manner that does not allow the target to fire back, at least not with any accuracy. This can work very well when you detect skepticism that has not yet been expressed. Make a preemptive strike when you know what's causing the person to doubt you.

- **Counterfire.** Firing back after an assault may actually trigger back-and-forth firing, so you may feel more comfortable thinking of this tactic as fencing rather than shooting. For example, in your role as the Interrogator, you might have someone challenge the solution to the problem that you've arrived at. There are lots of ways to fire back and throw the advantage back to your side, including something like, "The boss pulled off a move like this in his last company and saved $4 million in maintenance costs." With this tactic, you have to be ready to continue the repartee.

In the context of gaining acceptance as an expert, tactics force your audience into position, so that you can get them on track for what you want, that is, your desired outcome. You use tactics when skeptics take action that puts you at risk, which is why I explore the use of them in depth in Chapter 10, Rescue Schemes.

PUTTING THE CONCEPTS TO WORK

The central theme of all of these strategies, techniques, and tactics is finding ways to communicate the relevance of what you know to the people in your audience, and then highlighting that relevance if they don't recognize it immediately. And trust me, sometimes they will not, even when it should be obvious, because they are too self-absorbed. If that's the case, an integral part of succeeding as an expert is shifting their attention outward.

One company where I had been brought in to do project management consulting asked me to participate in a systems integration discussion as one of my first meetings. Each person at the meeting was so focused on what the subject meant to him that they had all lost sight of what the project meant to the company, much less to the others in the group. The real magic of being an expert is taking what a subject means to an individual and making it mean something to everybody. If it's just about you, you don't need to be an expert. In this case, I sat quietly, absorbed the key issues, and made the correlations in my head. At that point, I jumped in with links between concerns and solutions, perceptions on common ground, and insights into going forward as a team.

Just as I did in this instance, you can come across with a lot of power—and gain immediate acceptance as an expert—when you're the one who makes each person feel like he helped to score the winning run. As he tastes the Stone Soup and reflects on how good it tastes, his ingredient is always the most palatable—and he knows that everyone else can taste it, too. If you had not made the soup, he would not have had that opportunity.

THE ROLE AND SHAPE OF RESEARCH

¤ ¤ ¤

In interrogation, all activities start with an assessment of collection requirements. The type of research that ensues reflects those requirements.

If I go into a compound knowing that it's my job to find the chemical weapons expert and discover recent activities in that field, those requirements focus my planning and preparation on a narrow band of information. Lacking that information, I would wander in like an ignorant hick and ask, "Y'all don't have any chemical weapons, do ya?" But armed with some information about the person I'm talking to combined with a few bright stripes of information about the subject, I can artfully control the conversation. I inject the information at precisely the right times to remove all doubt that I, as well, am an expert.

This chapter will teach you how to learn in short order what matters to the person or people you will be talking to, how to know what kind of information gets priority attention, and how to vet sources of information.

To start, I want to give you three examples of research gone awry: how the failures related to the audience, what information should have received priority attention, and flawed sources of information. I'll also give you some initial insights on how these failures could have been averted.

A man showed up at a Mormon Deseret Industries farm after doing a little research about the church and thought he knew enough to get accepted. In exchange for work at one of these farms, the Mormon Church will feed you, put money in the bank for you, and help you get back on your feet. In the initial interview, someone asked this man the most basic question: "Are you a member of the church?" He said, "Yes. I'm an Eighty."

His answer showed two defects in his research and one in the way he used it. The latter is obvious: He should have stuck with what he had learned instead of extrapolating. The guy had heard of the Seventy, modeled after the New Testament Quorum of the Seventy, so he'd thought he go one better and be an Eighty.

The research itself had two problems. First, his audience was people who want to help a fellow church member; this is a kindness and a service centered on personal connections, on being part of the church family. Knowing facts about the church without having any names or personal references immediately put him at a disadvantage. Second, a bulleted list of facts about the church or a couple of paragraphs summarizing church structure is about as useful as the statistics memorized by an autistic savant like Dustin Hoffman's Raymond Babbitt. He did research, but he didn't have the right package of information.

It would have been better for him to say that a former neighbor of his, who was a Seventy, had introduced him to the church a little while back. That would give him real power because he would be affiliated with someone who is an expert. If you are trying to enter a very regimented group, such as the Mormon Church, you are much better off going the route of associating yourself with someone who is already there, rather than trying to break in through other means. In fact, Mormons love converts, so all he would have had to say was, "I am interested." His research was poorly focused and included elements of his own desire to be better, so it resulted in projection.

The second example involved embarrassment for an entire entourage that had been brought in to close a deal with the senior member of a Taiwanese company. The founder of a start-up company, a nontechnical entrepreneur who had done a wonderful job of recruiting people with expertise in technology, had made an appointment with the founder of a Taiwanese company to discuss licensing his compression technology. The meeting location was a private area of a booth at an enormous computer show in Las Vegas. Upon arriving, the entrepreneur promptly sat down at the table and began talking business. "I don't want to waste your time," he began, "so I'll get right to the point." He was a smart man who seemed to grasp the nuances of the technical information his staff had given him, and he had even developed an impressive command of the jargon.

What's wrong with this picture? His research should have included what a senior Taiwanese business executive considers civilized behavior, namely, a proper greeting before commencing business, as well as the use of his title—"doctor." The team the entrepreneur had brought with him could see that the meeting was going nowhere, even though their boss said all the right things technically. At the end of the scheduled time, their Taiwanese counterparts politely said good-bye, and that was the last anyone heard from them. Basically, the boss had asked the wrong people to brief him. He probably would have gotten a second shot at working out a deal with the company if he'd shown admiration and limited knowledge about the technology, an appropriate amount of deference to the host and his prized Ph.D., and keen attention to cultural priorities.

The third failure was a heartbeat away from success; this is the kind that you are more likely to experience that the other two. At the last minute, a popular keynote speaker at a conference of people in the publishing industry got sick. She e-mailed her slide presentation to a colleague, who had about two hours to prepare. He felt intense pressure because the audience knew this keynoter well and enjoyed her quirky slides and off-the-cuff style.

He stepped up to the podium and admitted that he had a lot of blanks to fill in because the speaker had supplied him with slides, but few notes. Proceeding through the slides, he did reasonably well until he got to the picture of a crossword puzzle. "I have no idea what this is doing here," he said disarmingly. People laughed with him, not at him, but one audience member spoke up and said, "She uses this to illustrate . . ." and then proceeded to explain the slide. After a couple more instances like this, the speaker just advanced to the next slide, not even bothering to mention the fact that he had no idea what a particular slide meant.

Although the audience found some benefit in the presentation, the understudy did not shine. No one mistook him for an expert.

What he should have done was a combination of two things: (1) use the research time available to determine which slides represented major concepts, and therefore merited more time, and (2) during the presentation, use the audience's knowledge of the material and familiarity with the scheduled keynoter's presentation style to his advantage. In a sense, the interactive nature of the resulting presentation would have positioned him as the expert who regulated the flow of the presentation, but the audience would have essentially given the keynoter's presentation to one another in a workshop format. And what do you call that? Stone Soup.

MATCHING INFORMATION AND AUDIENCE

Before I go into an interrogation, I get whatever personal effects the prisoner has carried with him. Let's say he has almost no money, no cigarettes or matches, a few pieces of standard-issue clothing, and a wallet full of photos. To an interrogator, there's no such thing as nonpertinent information, so I'm going to look at every button and every scrap of paper. I see that the photos are pictures of his wife and kids over the past few years. Before I ever talk with him about his role in the battlefield or what kind of intelligence he can provide me, I build rapport with him by getting him to talk about his family.

Common sense, you think. Yes, it is. But it's the same common sense about the audience that the CEO of that start-up company missed when he met with the Taiwanese businessman. It's also the piece that the wannabe Mormon and the understudy presenter missed: Not one of them started his research with a focus on the audience.

Most people I've talked with over the years, including some supposedly well-informed hosts of TV news shows, make the assumption that interrogators direct the conversation. Usually, that is not what happens. We operate with *source-directed requirements.*

A source-directed interview—and this is an extremely effective approach to job interviewing that I have used as a consultant—is one in which you simply get the other person to talk while you look for stress, pleasantness, and other discrete responses, and then you follow up on that. By doing this, you find out what's important to the person, what makes her nervous, what makes her happy. This is the process of following source leads.

Source leads can be:

- **Written**: e-mails, web site, checkbook record, notes. What do you know about someone who inserts emoticons into every e-mail? That's a person who has concerns about being misunderstood.

- **Physical**: clothing, car, gadgets. No matter what anyone says, nobody drives a Corvette because it's a practical car. So when you find the answer to the question, "Why do you drive a Corvette?" you have gotten inside someone's head.

- **Spoken**: jargon, pitch, tone, cadence. Signs of strain in the voice and rambling in response to a straightforward question can be signs of nervousness, but if you detect a slowing cadence and soft tones, the lead you follow can relate to physical attraction, or at least admiration. All of the jargon you learned in research has to be tuned for the audience, so understanding the person you are talking to is imperative to prevent you from stumbling around, awkwardly muttering technical terms. New consultants often make this mistake. The new consultant learns so much about the customer that she wants to impress the customer with what she knows. So she starts the minute she meets the receptionist. The receptionist looks at her as though she has extra eyes. She is, after all, in the people business and not the electronics business.

PRIORITY INFORMATION

When you're new to a topic, you need ways of determining:

- **Core concepts**. In your Web research, look for the hyperlinks. Particularly in Wikipedia, the hyperlinks are keywords. In regular text or oral presentations, such as lectures and news broadcasts, pay attention to nouns. There is a joke that TV news anchors have lost their verbs. They say things like, "Gambling. Washington, DC. U.S. Capitol building. News at 9."

- **Hot news related to the topic**. I was in a meeting recently where the conversation turned to baseball and the arcane information got stifling. One of the female executives at the table adeptly turned the topic toward current events. "Looks like Joe Torre won't have a job with the Yankees much longer" was all she had to say to gain a lot of buy-in from the baseball fanatics. She was a news junkie, not a sports junkie, but she knew how to adapt what she knew to the conversation. News always constitutes priority information.

- **What elements of the topic strike a chord with people**. Immediately go to the sponsored links on Google or one of the other search engines. They will lead you quickly to sites that reflect market research, that is, web sites that highlight what matters to people, what they find interesting and appealing. (Important note: You need to combine what you learn in this section with the guidance on vetting given in the next section, because together, they give you the whole picture of what constitutes valuable research from the perspective of both facts and appeal.) Keep a high-level view of the information you find on these sponsored sites. Don't go down the rabbit hole that the organization's marketing people want to take you down. Use the information they highlight because it will show you what they have determined are the pain points about the issue.

  You can do this with anything from technology to noodles. Type in "computer hardware" and the top sponsored link will first tell you what kinds of hardware are available—with pictures—and then tell you how you can save money on them. You find out immediately how to gratify your desires and reduce your pain. Type in "soba noodles" and the top sponsored link will tell you why they are so good, what to do with them, and how to buy them at a discount. Again, no pain, only gain.

  To sum it up, the logic behind relying on sponsored links is that you use the expertise of the companies and organizations to give you the human side of the topic immediately, then vet the source after you have exploited its market research.

I chose a topic that I then explored with the idea of priority information in mind. It was "AIDS in Africa."

The top site starkly presented a page of statistics about the ravaging effects of AIDS/HIV. Based on what I've already told you about how statistics should be used, but usually aren't, this is a page of logic disasters. It tells you such things as how many people have died from the disease in a particular part of Africa, but not how many people live there; how many women have the disease, but not how that number relates to any other population statistic. It throws out a lot of numbers, but notes the source of only one of them.

But here is why it does a great job and would serve you well in determining priority information. *Forget the actual numbers* and focus on the subject areas. This is a site that aims to get your financial support for AIDS/HIV research and treatment, so the information covers key areas for "people who care." It gives you a *frame of reference* for exploring the primary concerns related to the topic, that is, the magnitude of the problem and the types of populations that have been affected. Specifically:

- Millions of people worldwide have died.

- Millions are living with the disease, and about three-quarters of them are living in Africa.

- This is a big problem for women as well as men.

- The geographic areas of greatest growth for the disease are Ethiopia, Nigeria, China, India, and Russia.

- There is a high rate of new infections.

- The target population is young people.

- The disease creates millions of orphans.

As I said, you can forget the actual numbers. If you are doing basic research, you take the areas highlighted on this home page and hop out of it having armed yourself with the knowledge of what kinds of facts rivet the attention of people who follow this problem.

If the role you want to adopt is "expert by statistics," then this is the wrong way to go and the wrong site to visit. This is a site that gives you snapshots for the explicit purpose of arousing your emotions and enlisting your financial support. Take it for what it is.

This is priority information because you need to know these numbers (i.e., degrees of magnitude) and key concerns in order to have a framework for understanding the impact of AIDS/HIV in the world. This kind of information—flawed as it is from a healthy skeptic's perspective—gives you the substance you need to do additional research, or simply to launch an intelligent discussion of the topic in a way that invites others to contribute (the Pearl, Stone Soup, and so on).

VETTING THE SOURCE

The following guidance applies to both written and spoken information. In every case, you start with the assumption that what you are about to read or hear cannot be taken at face value.

MOTIVATION

In looking at the types of information I covered in Chapter 5— descriptive, anecdotal, statistical, and opinionated—you might quickly conclude that it's only the last one that motivation has a major role in shaping. Not so. Motivation can profoundly affect all of them.

You've just found out that your sister-in-law, whom you're about to visit, has been diagnosed with lymphoma. You have a couple of hours, and you have decided to use them to become familiar with treatments. Your first step is an Internet search for descriptive information.

"Lymphoma treatments" brings up millions of hits. You decide to ignore the .com sponsored links, thinking that their motivation must be to sell something, and proceed to the sites below them.

At the first one, a so-called information network, you learn that radiation, chemotherapy, immunotherapy, and bone marrow transplant are the treatments. The second site is a .gov that mentions all of these, plus two experimental treatments. The next one mentions surgery, too; it's a physician-sponsored site. The next one gets into some fairly technical nomenclature to describe various options, and the advice keeps looping back to conversations with your oncologist. The wow factor is high, so you go to "About Us" to find out the brains behind this operation. It's physicians whose articles are peer reviewed, as well as reviewed by a Pharm.D. (that is, a Doctor of Pharmacy). You continue your search, and you see the same kind of treatment information repeated over and over on multiple sites.

You conclude that the motivation behind all these web sites is to help people get the disease into remission by telling them about radiation, chemotherapy, immunotherapy, transplants, and surgery.

But wait. What about natural treatments? A quick search yields almost nothing because, as you soon find out, the preferred phrase in this arena is "natural cures," not "natural treatments."

You conclude that the motivation behind all of these web sites is to help people use herbs, minerals, energy balancing, the law of attraction, and so on to eliminate the disease.

Anyone in his right mind would rather get rid of the problem than manage it. If you are new to the world of lymphoma, therefore, you are likely to be swayed by the motivation of the natural cures folks.

Anecdotal information, which you look at next, comes from people who want you to know what worked and what didn't work. Their motivation, for the most part, is to save you time, money, and aggravation in dealing with a shared problem. Unless you're a natural skeptic, you could easily be swayed by dramatic stories of how raw vegetables and long walks in the park cured the disease in three months.

Finally, statistics ought to be as emotionally untainted as the result you get when you balance your checkbook. They are what they are. In this case, however, statistical information might be shaped by the desire to hook you on a particular course of treatment or natural cure. What's wrong with a statistic that asserts that more people are in remission as a result of chemotherapy and radiation than of minerals and positive thinking? For one thing, our society keeps statistics on people who undergo the first two treatments, but the information on the second group is largely anecdotal. A second point is that, even if we did have records on both, in the United States it is still uncommon for people to think of minerals and positive thinking as the sole ways of dealing with a serious illness. Which way is correct?

You've just spent an hour absorbing conflicting information from people who are highly motivated to pull you in opposite directions. You sought descriptive information, but what you actually got is what you often get with descriptive information: opinionated descriptions. Ask yourself these basic questions when considering motivation:

1. *What is the natural inclination of your source?* Like your audience, you may or may not know the web site host or the author of the book. Still, you can ask yourself a logical question: Why did this person create this site or write this book? As you look at the credits on the site, you find out that his mother died of lymphoma when he was a child and that he has since been diagnosed and is living with the disease. That tells you a bit about his inclination. If the web site creator is a drug vendor, you know something about the corporation's natural inclinations as well.

2. *What does the source need?* No one does a web page or writes a book without some motive. Whether it is a dedication to

someone, a need to be recognized as an expert, or for financial gain, ask yourself: What does this source need from *me*?

3. *What does the source stand to lose?* As you read the information, ask yourself whether broadcasting totally false information will cost the source anything. Is there a likely legal ramification from his swearing to have seen Elvis and Jimmy Hoffa gambling in Atlantic City? What about selling cures for cancer online? There is a reason why most diploma mills and unlicensed Viagra dealers use e-mail to market: It makes them harder to trace than if they set up shop downtown. When you are dealing with information, ask yourself: Do I have a good reason to believe this? Does anyone?

4. *What does the source stand to gain?* Some web sites get paid for the amount of traffic they redirect to another site. Remember this as you visit web sites with high numbers of pop-ups and redirects. Also remember that some people may feel that they are helping you when they give you garbage information that they have learned from another source. Their motivation is good, but their judgment is bad. Do you recognize the type? That's right: the sponge.

Always verify.

Trust no one.

Ask the tough question: If I'm having a hard time believing this, will anyone believe it?

ANOMALIES

Did you see anything in the information that strikes you as odd? Hint: Following hyperlinks and actually reading source material will sometimes point you toward irregularities.

The first anomaly to surface is the blanket assertion that cancer mortality rates in Sri Lanka, China, and Japan are much lower than those in the United States because of the Asian diet. It turns out that while that's true for certain types of cancer, when it comes to liver, stomach, and esophageal cancer, you see much higher death rates in China and Japan than in the United States. So you wonder: Maybe what they're saying about diets isn't correct, or at least it's not the only major factor that's operating. So what else are they missing?

Flip back to one of the Western medicine web sites and go through the same exercise. Page after page seems airtight, consistent, well documented, and compelling. There are no discernible anomalies until you track down some of the sources of information about chemotherapy. In one search, a suspicious 6 references out of 27 about the efficacy of chemo came from a single pharmaceutical company.

Ten minutes spent looking for anomalies has now raised issues for you about the reliability of the information coming from both camps. Chinks in the armor.

So who is right? Remember that the outcome you need drives your research. You may in fact discover enough information in your two hours to ask the toughest questions a doctor has ever heard and, in fact, have the ability to use the Interrogator strategy to extract things from the doctor that he himself has not even considered.

SIMPLICITY/COMPLEXITY

Going back to the discussion of motivation, I want to point out that if the mission of authors of lymphoma treatment information is indeed to help consumers, then they should use the language of consumers. This is a simple matter of designing your information to suit your audience. When a site that is ostensibly designed for consumers peppers its explanations of treatment protocols with jargon, you have to wonder: Are they trying to help me, or to force me to call my doctor or my local pharmacist for an explanation?

Here's the rub. When you actually go to a doctor's office, is the doctor the one who actually translates the jargon for you? Not in many cases. As he occupies his mind with more and more of the minutiae of his specialty, he has a harder time relating his information to average people. Think about the last time you had to see a specialist about a medical problem. The ability to rely on interpreters—physician's assistants, nurses, receptionists, patient advocates—gives many doctors permission to use thousand-dollar words when ten-cent words would help them actually communicate with patients. Remember this when you are using the Interrogator strategy: You have the right to, and can, ask defining questions for your own edification and that of others.

It's no surprise, then, that the lymphoma treatment discussions on web sites dominated by physician input have a level of complexity that does not match the vocabulary of many patients. At sites like this, you experience the tactic of barraging in order to reinforce expertise—the ever-present language of those closer to The One.

Moving to the information provided by the "opposing" camp, you notice an abundance of simple, clear explanations of why natural cures work. They are often so simple, in fact, that an old adage comes to mind: "If it sounds too good to be true, then it probably is." But they do a great job of getting you emotionally charged about the patient's ability to control her situation and cure herself. Remember that this level of simplicity is driven by the other extreme: people who have little or no exposure to the information and learning of the initiates of medicine. They are playing on your sense of loss of control to convince you that there is a better way. Most of these pages rely purely on anecdotes and give little clinical evidence.

Interestingly enough, information from both "sides" is likely to trigger an emotional response: One side arouses a sense of inadequacy and dependence as the threshold emotions for being hopeful, and the other arouses a take-charge optimism.

This look at the way the information providers use simplicity and complexity to present their cases may well drive you to revisit the motivation conclusions you had before. These people may be trying to help, but is that their primary or their secondary agenda? Do they want to prove that their approach to treatment is right more than they want to help people?

You are now about 90 minutes into your research and somewhat discouraged about the quality of the information available.

FALSE COGNATES

For a moment, I'm going to move away, but only slightly, from the research scenario to explore the idea of false cognates. Right now, think of the definition of two words: *event* and *ton*.

What's an event?

- A calendar object that is commonly used to represent things that mark time or use time (CalConnect).

- An action or occurrence detected by a program. Events can be user actions, such as clicking a mouse button or pressing a key, or system occurrences, such as running out of memory (Webopedia).

- A social occasion or activity (Merriam-Webster).

- Individual sports contest: a race or other competition that forms part of a larger sports occasion such as the Olympic Games (msn Encarta).

- The fundamental observational entity in relativity theory (wordnet.princeton.edu).

- An event in particle physics describes one set of particle interactions occurring in a brief span of time, typically recorded together (Wikipedia).

- What precipitates a play. For example, Big Daddy's birthday is the event in *Cat on a Hot Tin Roof* (screenwriting.info).

- An event is an interpretation of a tuple. While a tuple is simply a data structure, an event corresponds to something in the real world (streambase.com).

- An "event" in genetic engineering is the insertion of a particular piece of foreign DNA into the chromosome of the recipient (pioneer.com).

And it goes on and on and on, from field to stream. So if you see the word *event* on a web site devoted to lymphoma treatments, do you really know if it refers to an appointment with a doctor, an experimental therapy, or an invitation to a fundraiser? The context should give you the answer, but consider the potential confusion over *ton*.

It's weight, right? Not if you're talking about air conditioning. In that context, it has to do with capacity as it relates to cooling power. So if you're buying an air conditioner and you find out that the cost corresponds to tons, don't be concerned.

You are not stupid if you hit a word that has both a common usage and a subject-specific one, and you don't know what it means. High-quality information, both in written and in spoken form, will give you a definition of such a word up front. This is not an insult; it is a sign that the motivation—again, that's a major driver—is to communicate with you rather than manipulate you.

With this in mind, you revisit some of the key sites and realize that common words like *salvage* and *maintenance* have meanings unique to the treatment discussion.

You've spent two hours researching the topic of lymphoma treatment, but even after having vetted the sources carefully, you wonder about your expertise.

CONCLUSION OF SCENARIO

Should your sister-in-law now accept you as an expert who can help her improve, and even save, her life? Yes, with the caveat that you are a guide to help her get the right answers, not a medical professional. After just two hours of research, you can answer three major questions:

- What information is beneficial, or at least does no harm? Lifestyle information: eating and exercising to improve the immune system, positive thinking.

- What information requires probing by a skeptical mind? Anything about treatments and cures. Especially if your sister-in-law is a sponge, she needs to have a skeptic by her side who is ready to ask tough questions and to listen with objectivity. (Maybe that can now be you.) You are prepared to ask the doctor some of the toughest questions he has ever heard.

- What information is seriously flawed, or even bogus? Most of the advice that begins, "This is the only way."

On one level, those answers sound like common sense, but the research gives your answers depth. You now have the ability to refer to specific resources, target the controversies about treatments, and point to red flags, among other things. You aren't just coming up with comments that make sense; you are a well-informed source of guidance.

Most importantly, you have matched what you learned to the needs of your audience. Your sister-in-law wouldn't need any medical assistance if you had all the answers. By learning what you did and helping her sort information into those three categories, you provided the intersection of information and human requirements—that is, expertise. Now she is prepared to tackle the specialists.

CASE STUDIES IN RESEARCH

I've chosen two very different topics to illustrate how to conduct research with a focus on the audience, a sense of priorities, and proper vetting.

CASE STUDY 1 : REINDEER FARMING

The expert challenge: A person I met at a horse auction, which is somewhere I'm likely to go, invited me to meet some very important people who are highly successful reindeer farmers. I have enough time between meeting this person and going to the event to change my clothes and do a Web search.

- Research time: 15 minutes

- Duration of time with the audience: 1 hour

- Audience: Wealthy reindeer farmers

- Desired outcome: Get them to hire me as the worldwide spokesman for reindeer farmers

- Background assets: Expertise about human behavior; knowledge about horses, which I raise

- Plan of attack: Research the basics and focus on areas that connect to my knowledge base as someone who raises horses

Where do I get my information?

- Google provides 663 sites with the discrete phrase "reindeer farming" in .16 seconds. (That's less time than it took for you to read this bullet point. Of course, you have to add the five seconds it took for me to type in the phrase.)

- I refine the search further by indicating that the site must include the word "products" and be in English. It's my plan that this will point me to sites that focus on the business considerations related to reindeer farming. That search takes 0.8 seconds, and the yield is now down to 254 sites.

- In five minutes, I scan the top sites produced by associations, government information sources, and people in the business. I see the word "genetics," which leads to a discussion of "artificial insemination," and I realize that I'm in familiar territory. I have to know these things to breed horses.

- Within two more minutes, I realize that reindeer farmers have the same artificial insemination (AI) issues that I do, so we can talk shop.

- I quickly go back to a Google news search for recent articles on "reindeer," so that I know the buzz. In two seconds, I get a ridiculous collection of about 200 articles that I scan quickly. Most of them are irrelevant, except that I see one on an unfortunate situation—a potential "nightmare before Christmas"—in Scotland, where reindeer have been afflicted with foot and mouth and blue tongue disease. Here's a hook: I now have a question to ask of the reindeer farmers that will get them throwing around their expertise and debating information that should tell me a lot more about the business. It's a basic "tell me more."

What this less than 15 minutes of research enables me to do is get to the heart of sounding smart with someone: If you know what keeps a person awake at night and can commiserate with him on those topics, then to him, you're a genius. My group of reindeer farmers meeting in upstate New York may have to deal with the ugly disease that keeps Santa's usual escorts from appearing in a parade. There will be some disease issues that they have to deal with—and if they have a disease-free herd, you can be assured that they want you to know it.

This is an issue that easily leads back to something I know about, which is breeding animals for health and aesthetics. So, in one hour, I use the Spider to connect the conversation to what I know through both comments and questions. I adapt what the audience members say about reindeer to my experiences as a horse farmer, and when their conversation doesn't lead to it naturally, I ask a question that will invariably allow me to accomplish that task. I also rely a bit on the Pearl to glean information as we speak, and roll that into my understanding of the business.

What if your expertise includes business opportunities—say, you have an MBA in marketing—but you know nothing about animals? Your research might lead you to focus on the "deer urine market" or the "antler felt market" so that you could ask questions about the purported profitability of these products.

CASE STUDY 2: BASEBALL

The expert challenge: A man and a woman who know very little about the great American pastime want to close a deal with someone who is a baseball fanatic.

- Research time: 30 minutes

- Audience: A prospective client

- Desired outcome: Establish strong, positive rapport with the client to get an edge over the other design firm vying for a big job. After all, sales is about you

- Background assets: Growing up in the United States; a good education

- Plan of attack: Do enough research to make sense out of what's in the news

Where do they get their information?

- The starting point is espn.com to blast them with jargon and unintelligible summaries of key plays in the final game of the 2007 National League Championship Series between the Colorado Rockies and the Arizona Diamondbacks. Their objective is to understand everything they are reading on that page—and more—with their half-hour of research and conversation.

- They see this chart and scratch their heads:

.254	BA	.222
8	R	18
0	SB	2
2	HR	3
39	K	28
3.00	ERA	1.89

They know they need to apply knowledge that is universal and not dependent on the topic, so they follow a logical analytical process. The points that are immediately apparent by knowing something about numbers in general are:

- The first number must be a proportion; they don't know if higher or lower is better.

- The next three whole numbers are probably absolutes; since it's a game involving scoring, the higher numbers are likely to be better.

- The last number shows a relationship, but it's not clear whether higher or lower is better.

- They begin reading the story, which is a compilation of five "series notes," or bulleted game highlights of about 40 words each. It's mostly gibberish, but parsing the sentences makes the following points apparent:

- The Rockies accomplished two firsts: This is the first time they played in the World Series, and they were the first team in 31 years to win their first seven games ever in post-season play.

- ○ Someone named Seth Smith did something good that he had never done during regular season play.

- ○ Matt Holliday's performance made a big difference to the Rockies in winning their playoff games. For his sake, let's hope he plays for the Rockies.

- ○ Kaz Matsui did a lot of something called an RBI, which appears to be good.

- ○ Conor Jackson made errors that were good for the Rockies, so he must be a player for the other side.

So even without reading about this strange sport called baseball, the two novices have some basic information that could suggest interest in this particular game, at least, if not the sport as a whole.

- • With only 20 minutes left, turning to Wikipedia is a good bet. The novices first check to see whether this is a vetted article or something flagged as having a lot of undocumented information. Their hope is that in 20 minutes, they can get at least enough information to build on the five points in the original article about the playoff game.

- • They need to focus on hyperlinks to see what the priority concepts are. The first paragraph seems to be straightforward English, with hyperlinks calling attention to transparent concepts, such as hits and runs. Only one hyperlinked concept jumps out as confusing: errors. They don't want to fall into the trap of false cognates (described earlier), so they want to verify that errors are, indeed, mistakes. They click on the word and quickly confirm that their assumption about Conor

Jackson being from the other team was correct—his mistakes (errors) helped the Rockies.

- The next useful hyperlinks are the ones that give a rundown on the current teams in the two leagues. That gives them a sense of what else is out there, but since the client's favorite team is the Rockies, that's the only one that merits focus.

- Failing to see any hyperlinks that explain the letters with the statistics, they do a search for "baseball jargon" and find another Wikipedia site, which gives them exactly what they need.

- They return to the five bullet points of the earlier story and put that information together with their newfound understanding of the stats. One important discovery: The statistics in the box couldn't possibly apply to the single game described in the story. They give a picture of what happened in the series of games between the two teams; therefore, they provide a lot of fodder for discussing the playoffs.

- Returning to espn.com, they figure that the one additional thing they should know is what the headline news in the sport is, besides this Rockies victory. They learn that Joe Torre will not be returning as manager of the Yankees.

The pair is now ready for the meeting.

INFORMATION OVERLOAD

You have just spent two hours looking up information that not only was shaped by your audience and your intended outcome, but also considers the duration of your session. You need to decide how all of this fits into your strategy and how you will use it along with techniques to establish yourself. When you walk into the room with all of your newfound knowledge, will you be like the new consultant and start to spray the room with disjointed facts? Or will you take a cool and measured approach that delivers on your knowledge?

No matter how much data you learn in your directed study, it is still just information—it's nothing more than a database of facts and figures until you establish relationships among the bits and pieces. You need to learn to package information to deliver it effectively instead of either holding a mound of information and handing it over in a lump or arbitrarily grabbing little pieces of it and tossing it, like throwing stones at your audience. Your next skill, then, is packaging.

CHAPTER

7

PACKAGING INFORMATION

¤ ¤ ¤

In her *Parade* magazine column, Marilyn vos Savant regularly runs word and number puzzles like this one that appeared on October 7, 2007: What do these letter combinations have in common? BLL, LST, MSS, PCK. You may look at them and know the answer instantly, because you're good with words as well as with patterns. The relationships among things jump out at you. If so, then you have a natural ability to package information so as to present yourself as an expert, and, as a corollary, you probably find it easier to learn a range of concepts because you see how they fit with your existing knowledge base. If you are such a person, then you saw immediately that all of these letter combinations can be turned into words with any vowel except the occasional vowel Y.

If you aren't such a person, don't worry about it. I'm about to give you some methods of packaging information that will sharpen your ability to see patterns and relationships. They will also help you exploit the natural tendency of humans to group words in a way that educates an active listener.

Use the following principles to make correlations and to eliminate complexities that can get in the way of understanding core concepts:

- Families of information

- Parsing

- Rules of thumb

- Christmas tree

- Allegory

In different ways, all these principles will help you learn a new subject area more easily, as well as convey your newfound expertise to others. You will hone your skill in making real connections between bits of data, rather than just regurgitating a lot of facts.

As with strategies, techniques, and tactics, you need to be mindful of your audience in using these ways to package information. People who have an engineer's or an investigator's brain (both technicians) want to go from A to B to C in learning information and will not respond well to allegory, which presents information in a broad way and invites the listener to fill in the details. You have to take the audience's style into consideration, even if it's not yours, if you want to be perceived as an expert.

FAMILIES OF INFORMATION

We'll start by playing *Jeopardy*, the game in which you are given the answer, but you have to provide the question.

Answer: Twelve

Question: How many eggs in a dozen? How many inches in a foot?

Sorry. It's "How many Apostles were there?"

I can see that you wouldn't think that was fair because you didn't have a category to guide your response. A category in *Jeopardy* expresses a family of information. You can have thousands of facts memorized, but if you cannot connect what you know to the family of information presented—in the case of the game show, within seconds—then you cannot give the correct response. For example, how many well-schooled people would freeze if the category were Tragic American History, and the answer was Abraham Lincoln? One contestant might hit the buzzer and say, "Who was the sixteenth president of the United States?" Wrong. Another might hit the buzzer and say, "Who issued the Emancipation Proclamation?" Wrong. Realizing what category, or family of information, she was in, the third contestant would hit the buzzer and say, "Who was the first American president to be assassinated?" Correct.

The principle of families of information can help you present expertise using any strategy. Here's an example using the broad category of "domesticated animal."

You're at a business event, and a few people, including a prospective client, are having a conversation about the cute tricks their dogs can do. You'd like to move to slightly more serious ground so that you can come across as well informed. You mention that you have friends who think their alpacas make better pets than dogs. "They're domesticated animals?" someone questions. You reply, "Oh, yes. My friend Marsha told me they've been domesticated for thousands of years. She raises suri alpacas." "Suri? As in Katie Holmes's and Tom Cruise's daughter?" another person asks incredulously. "Yep. Just like that. In fact, after she was born, my friends sent them a blanket made out of suri hair." Someone then observes that it's a little odd to name your kid after an animal. Now you have your opening: "Actually, it's Persian for Red Rose, and names like this are becoming less strange. I read an article in the *Wall Street Journal* a few months ago saying that sociologists have seen a dramatic rise in the anxiety that people have over naming their children." You've successfully used the Spider to take the conversation from Fido's fetching routines to current events— knowledge you are intimate with. Does the transition seem awkward? Not if it's done correctly. You are relying on source leads to get you where you need to be.

EXERCISE: FAMILIES BIG AND SMALL

Complete this table with additional options on families of information into which the topic on the left can fit.

Tires	Cars Rubber products
Weeds	Yard maintenance TV shows
Robert E. Lee	Famous military leaders Famous Broadway personalities

There are no right or wrong answers, only different ones. Now share your list with a friend and see what he comes up with. Are there surprises?

One caveat and warning regarding families of information: Your knowledge can become so specialized that everything seems to relate back to your specialization. This relationship could be true, or it could be that you are projecting (in the standard, psychology-based definition)—that is, seeing what you want to see. If you do that, you are acting like the Vanderbilt lady, so be cautious.

PARSING

The skill of parsing is language-centered. Merriam-Webster defines "to parse" as "to resolve (as a sentence) into component parts of speech and describe them grammatically." In the old days, English teachers taught parsing by having students diagram sentences. I had my experiences with this in the mid-seventies with a very "proppah" southern "grammah teacher" who also was in her mid-seventies. I've yet to find someone in school today who knows how to diagram sentences, but it's a valuable skill if you want to sort through a complicated sentence because diagramming—whether you do it on paper or mentally—forces you to look at the relationship of words so that you can make sense out of the whole.

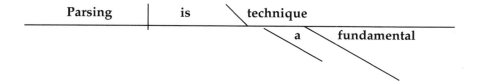

Parsing is a fundamental analytical technique that will help you clean up the way you absorb and express any kind of information. It will help you get to the core concepts of new information, spot the flaws in someone else's logic, and package your information with precision.

Maryann and I ran each other, and other people, through many "tests" related to breaking information into component parts. In one case, I said, "Throw me a topic you think I know nothing about and let me see if I can give you an intelligent response without looking anything up." Maryann said, "Leaf area index," a topic she'd edited a paper about a few years ago. I fought my initial impulse—a common one—to focus on the most familiar words and blow past anything else. If I had done that, I would have come up with some bogus explanation about the size of one kind of leaf versus another. But I took a second look and realized that "leaf area" modified the noun "index," so we had to be talking about something more encompassing than a couple of leaves. I speculated that we were talking about changes in vegetation in a particular area—a correct conclusion.

You can rely on a basic understanding of language usage and, instead of becoming my septuagenarian grammar teacher, simply apply what you know. Take the sentence apart and look for the key areas. If you are face to face, pay attention to what the person emphasizes. If the sentence is in written form, look for the intended targets of adjectives and adverbs. Look for the reuse of key words in other contexts to better understand how one word relates to the other. By doing this, you can deconstruct even the most complex and arcane jargon.

Finally, do not be shaken by a person's use or overuse of complex language. Language is a tool of communication. If the person speaking is using language that is inappropriate for the audience, you can become an expert simply by using the mechanical skill of parsing to align his language to the audience he is talking to. This works well with the Interpreter and Interrogator strategies.

RULES OF THUMB

Rules of thumb are simply calculations that establish relationships. One interpretation of that phrase relates to tailors relying on the thumb measurement as the basis for rough calculations of wrist, neck, and waist measurements. The rule: Double the wrist mea-

EXERCISE: SUBJECT, VERB, WHATEVER

Visit a few .edu web sites and look for information about a topic that's completely foreign to you. Identify core concepts—even if they don't make sense to you—by simply looking for the basic parts of speech: subject, verb, object. Apply understanding of how these words relate to one another. Try to use and reuse context to determine exactly what each phrase means. Try not to use dictionaries or other tools. This will build your confidence in your ability to *shift on the fly*.

surement and you know the neck size, and double the neck measurement and you know how big the waist is. A rule of thumb often takes the form of statements such as the following:

For every mile you walk, you burn 100 calories.
and
If you walk a mile, then you burn 100 calories.

Rules of thumb are effective phrases for anchoring information in your head, or someone else's, and for buttressing an argument. If you're applying for a job, for example, you should walk in knowing that the standard work year is 2,000 hours, so the rule is that your wage per hour is your salary divided by 2,000. If you want $500 more than the boss is offering you, therefore, all you're asking for is a measly 25 cents more per hour.

Unless they take the if/then form, however, the two ideas may not actually be related. For example, I could say that for every person in my hometown, there are two books in the library. That may be true, but now you have two unrelated ideas stuck in your head because I've established a rule-of-thumb relationship. Is that relevant? It depends on the outcome I want to achieve.

My purpose in wanting to be accepted as an expert may be that I want you to contribute a substantial amount of money to AIDS/HIV research. I have an audience of affluent Americans in front of me, and I tell them that about 40,000 new infections occur each year in the United States. They think, "So what? That's not me." I then say that about 40,000 Americans die in car crashes every year. They think, "That could be me." So now I'm trying to set up a relationship that suggests that Americans in general have as much chance of contracting AIDS as they do of dying in an auto accident.

You already know the flaws in this argument, statistically speaking, if you read Chapter 5. One hole is that a much wider swath of the American population is at risk of dying in a car accident because hundreds of millions of people drive and ride in cars on a regular basis. The high-risk population for HIV/AIDS, on the other hand, can be defined by certain lifestyle characteristics and preexisting conditions.

That's not the point in setting this up as a rule of thumb. If you are challenged, you emphasize correctly that the absolute number spotlights the magnitude of the problem in both cases.

EXERCISE: NOT ALL THUMBS

Use your imagination to come up with rule-of-thumb relationships between concepts or items that seem unrelated. Here's some inspiration: During the first atomic bomb test, Enrico Fermi started dropping bits of paper on the floor. At first they fell straight down. When the blast wave reached him, however, the paper was displaced as it fell to the ground. He did a rough calculation of bomb energy yield based on the movement of the paper. So how could he relate this? For every x millimeters the paper moved, he could estimate ykT of force.

CHRISTMAS TREE

I intentionally use this analogy because an old friend and supervisor in the military, David Hastings, used it effectively to teach interrogators to use framework. A bare-bones approach is easier to build than full-blown concepts.

Framework and jargon are two main communication tools used to convey expertise. The Christmas tree principle involves giving your audience a solid, obvious framework for your information, and then "decorating the tree" sequentially with details like jargon.

Framework refers to an understanding of where certain types of data fit into the big picture. Seasoned public relations people tend to be very good at using this concept. A reporter calls with questions about the company's new software suite. From talking with colleagues in order to get the information she needs to write press releases, the PR person knows enough to field the call intelligently, answering all of the fundamental "w" questions: what the product is, why the company developed it, when it will be released, and where it will be used. By getting a list of the reporter's technical questions, she can then get back to him to "decorate the tree" or have a technical guru take over and do it.

Moving to the details often involves the use of jargon, so if you grasp the framework but aren't a subject-matter expert, you could have a hard time with this. However, you can get help from the person you are trying to impress with your expertise. Encourage him to answer some of his own questions. And then, if you notice bare spots on the tree—and you are pretty sure he does—bring the session to a close and come back to it when you have the details you need to finish the job.

The process of engaging people to add the decorations can be smooth if you've matched the method to the audience. To put it in Myers-Briggs terms, the Christmas tree works well with people who fall into the sensing (versus intuition) approach to information gathering. Sensors are people who buy into only what they can see, smell, touch, and taste. They typically go from beginning to end; they appreciate an A-to-Z process. Just keep them moving around the tree in a logical fashion, adding things as you go.

Humans learn best and incorporate new ideas best from epiphany rather than from training. Asking questions that lead people to understand concepts at their own pace therefore creates more meaningful and usable learning. The Christmas tree works well in allowing a nontechnician to guide technicians through a discovery process.

In a group, you can ask questions of people to get the entire group to decorate the tree. You present the tree and offer them a box of ornaments so that they can pick and choose according to "taste." Some people will surely add ornaments that they brought with them, but you have provided the framework, the process for decorating, and the essentials for getting the job done.

EXERCISE: RED AND GOLD BALLS

Pick a straightforward topic about which you know "all" the basics, such as "growing a lawn" or "cooking a chicken." Write down the framework of your expertise, and then research the topic as if you knew nothing about it. What details surface? What does your tree look like after you have hung all the new ornaments?

ALLEGORY

I use the term *allegory* broadly and loosely, mostly to call attention to the central role of metaphor in this method of packaging information. The term also includes comparisons that illustrate, "It's just like this." In using allegory, you might tell an actual story to present the big picture of your expertise, or you might just call up images that make your point vividly. It's Spencer Johnson's approach to conveying expertise in *Who Moved My Cheese?*

This is not a method you want to use with a room full of technicians that you've just met (as I suggested earlier, they're Christmas tree people). To put it in Myers-Briggs terms again, allegory works well for the Ns—those who favor intuition over sensing. They are comfortable with abstract or theoretical information; a good story could pull them toward you quickly.

Here's an example of someone who used a metaphor that alienated his audience instead of winning them over. The board of a lobbying organization promoted the CFO to the top position. He was a bright man and a quick study, but he sometimes tried to use images to explain concepts, and he usually did this badly. One of these times, he used silos to represent the distinct areas of information that the firm dealt with, and then he turned the borders of the silos into perforated lines to suggest how the new approach to databases would allow people to share information.

The executives in the meeting were horrified. The human resources people had no intention of sharing their information with lobbyists, who had no intention of sharing with event planning, and so on. "What's the point of having the silo if everything's going to leak out of it?" someone asked.

That wasn't what he had in mind, of course. His vision was just that the different departments could share applicable information, not everything in their databases—like a recipe using just the right amounts of this and that from each source to create soup.

His problem was that he had a finance brain. He was a technician, so his tendency was to compartmentalize information. Silos represented the way the company was structured, with no vision of the complexity of the larger operation. His mind could not see the overarching concept and understand why HR would not want folks who trade in information to have exposure to sensitive data. He did not see that, in practical terms, his plan meant pouring ingredients into a pot in equal measure, and that the result could only be a pot of ingredients—and that doesn't give you soup.

After seeing big-picture presentations from his colleagues at other companies (don't you love those executive conferences?) about breaking down barriers, he believed he could apply this to his company by simply moving to an open-data concept. He chose a packaging technique that ran counter to the way he thought naturally, so he failed miserably in the execution. If he had stuck with his natural understanding of sharing numbers with all people who have a need to know those numbers, he would have fared better.

In contrast, here is an effective use of allegory. When Maryann, in her role as a literary agent, goes to the annual Book Expo of America, she has to visit a lot of people very quickly. Even those editors that she has formal appointments with have limited time for meetings. Her meetings range from 5 minutes to about 20 minutes, unless she is in the final stages of negotiating a deal. The circumstances of BEA offer her a great opportunity to become an expert on each publishing house quickly, however. Each house's books are on display. She can pick up a book that is in the same genre as something she's pitching, set it down in front of the publisher's representatives, and say, "I'm talking about something *like this.*" It's a physical allegory, associated with something they already have in their head.

There are analogous opportunities—using something in the environment to illustrate your expertise—in myriad other circumstances. And they are especially useful if your time is limited to minutes—for example, on a sales call or in an abbreviated job interview with the head of a company who has to be somewhere else in ten minutes.

Zero in on the company's slogan, anchor the discussion in recent press coverage, or pull out the gadget the company makes so that it's clear that you not only know about the gadget, but also own it. Show that you know where it fits in the larger context of "like" things. You don't have to explain what you know because you can demonstrate that you know it through association.

SUMMARY

Packaging information means boiling it down to simple terms. Looking for common denominators. Using analytical tools to spot the relevance between one word and other, and one concept and

EXERCISE: BEDTIME STORIES

Take a difficult concept like rebuilding an engine or microfinancing models for Third World countries. Explain this concept as though you were going to help a five-year-old understand it. Use animals, cartoon characters, red and yellow blocks, the story from a TV show—whatever works.

another. Drawing pictures with your words to illustrate difficult concepts.

For your research, you need to package information in ways that are relevant to you. But as you move to delivery and how you will present this information, the issue is how you will transfer this information to others. So you may need to revisit the packages as you go. Remember: No plan survives the first contact with the enemy. So think about how you see these data and how another person might see them as you prepare.

I did an experiment with someone who knew nothing about air conditioning other than how to turn it on, to see if I could get her to grasp the basics of dehumidifying air. Instead of discussing temperature and relative humidity, I simply relied on the fact that she has a reasonable amount of intelligence and a lot of life experience. I said, "I'm going to put 500 glasses of ice on a big tray in your living room, and all the glasses have plastic wrap on top. If I have a drain to remove the water from the room that condenses on the outside of the glass, what happens to the room?" She concluded that you would dehumidify it. "Right," I said. "And why the plastic wrap?" She said that that the plastic would prevent any water in the glass from evaporating, so that you wouldn't be adding any moisture back into the atmosphere. Without explanation, she understood that pushing moist air through a cold coil would have the same effect. She quickly concluded that this must be why the air conditioner leaks water.

Depending on how she adds to and shares that knowledge, she now has a package to show her expertise about how air conditioning dehumidifies air.

PART

3

EXECUTION AND RESCUE

CHAPTER

8

DELIVERING THE GOODS

¤ ¤ ¤

The flow of an interrogation never varies. The five acts in this "theater for one" are:

- Establish control

- Establish rapport

- Run approach(es)

- Question

- Terminate

The model for your sessions is the same, although the nomenclature is slightly different. You will establish control and rapport, but your approaches are the strategies I outlined in Chapter 5. The questioning phase in an interrogation is when the interrogator extracts information (his desired outcome); in your case, it involves using techniques to support your acceptance as an expert (your desired outcome). An interrogator's challenge is to get a source who is under duress to accept her as an expert and talk to her because of that. You have a more complex exercise: to get normal people in normal situations to accept you as an expert and talk to you as such. For that reason, the five "acts" of your play have a little more subtext.

In previous chapters, I covered the first four acts in a theoretical way, but now I will give you guidance on application. Chapter 9 addresses termination in much more detail.

ESTABLISH CONTROL

Establishing control is the step you must take to make people receptive to the idea that you have credibility as an expert. It involves building a bridge from the known to the unknown so that you have a place in the conversation. For example, if you have worked in the mailroom for the past five years, people in your company have a preconceived notion of what you're worth ("the known"). The only way to counter that is to revise where they see you in the hierarchy ("the unknown"), and you begin that process by establishing control in a situation that allows you to expose your expertise.

All of the preparation you have done has made you familiar with your audience, let you know the time frame for your presentation, and allowed you to become clear on the desired outcome. These elements are the foundation for establishing control, but they don't tell you how to do it. The "how to" requires you to put your personality and body language to work.

ROLE, OR PERSONALITY OF THE MOMENT

You may think that "control" sounds too extreme, but when you deliberately use a role to form a connection with the person or people from whom you want acceptance as an expert, in my interrogator's book, that's establishing control.

In *The Guantanamo Guidebook*, a program I did for Channel 4 in the United Kingdom, professional interrogators simulated experiences that might occur with post-9/11 sources detained at Guantanamo Bay. With one of the volunteer detainees in the show, I chose to greet him in a way that the other interrogators had not: They called him by his number, but I called him by his name. By doing that, the role I established with him was one of an authoritarian who respected him. It gave him a sense of dignity and a (false) sense of hope that made him more inclined to talk with me than with the others. After that, my words to him connected with greater force than the instructions or requests from other interrogators.

In a recent meeting with corporate clients, I reinforced my persona as a hard-ass by talking about wrestling with a bear. A real Alaskan brown bear. It was a true story. I was 18, and the bear was part of a traveling show that came to Georgia, so my account was not as dramatic as a wilderness survival story, but I didn't have to tell them that part. I did, though. I explained that I was a skinny kid and the whole event lasted two minutes, and although that was longer than most who tried, it was absolutely comical. It allowed me to let my clients know that I have an adventurous spirit (most of them said that even in a cage, they would not try it). At the same time, it allowed me to become more human as I let them know a fact about myself that I rarely shared. It was a bridge to connect me to them in a way that they would not otherwise have seen.

Given the situation, what will your style be? How flexible are you? For the time being, let's assume that you are not flexible; you're the what-you-see-is-what-you-get guy who has been in the mailroom for five years. Your role may be that of the kid who pointed out that the emperor wasn't wearing new clothes; in fact, he wasn't wearing *any* clothes. How do people respond to you then? With deference, simply because you noticed something that they either did not or would not admit that they did. You have established a measure of control.

As *The Closer*, Kyra Sedgwick often begins an interrogation by presenting herself as an administrative person who just seems a little curious about what really happened and is quite concerned about the person. She gets the source comfortable with her and then blindsides him. You could do that, or you could come in stern, or energetic and open, or silent and attentive, and so on, depending on your role in the hierarchy and what you plan to do next. If you know that everyone in the room is suffering from the same pain—say, slumping sales—you might want to pursue the misery-loves-company course of action if your strategy is to come across eventually as the problem solver. You go down the same rabbit hole with the others, only to pull everyone out later.

BODY LANGUAGE/CONTROL

If you consider the reasons why someone accepts you as an expert that were given in Chapter 1—and I develop the discussion in this chapter—then your common sense will tell you that different types of body language might be linked to each. How could this play out at a meeting where you want to gain acceptance as an expert? You've walked into the room, and you want to take action to help you establish control.

- You stake out real estate at a meeting table by placing your supporting materials in a way that defines your space as larger than most people's. You are saying, "I'm the only one who knows what's going on." (You are isolating.)

- You sit next to the person with greatest authority who has endorsed you. (That's affiliation.)

- Your slide presentation is queued up and ready to go. (This could be demonstration, generalization, humanization, or adaptation.)

- You sit across from warring department heads, so that you are the apex of the triangle—the point at which their ideas converge. (The position for association.)

- You take a seat at the head of the table. (Intimidation.)

The key thing to remember here is that this bridge is an introduction to a new concept for your audience: you as expert. You do not need to establish that first, but you need to get a measure of first contact so that you do not remain "Bob the mailroom guy" and nothing more. You are "Bob the mailroom guy with something worthwhile to say." This doesn't assure you of acceptance, but it does give you the opportunity you need. If I as an interrogator never establish control, whether in a sympathetic or a stern posture, I cannot take the next step in the process.

ESTABLISH RAPPORT

Control is reaching out for connection; rapport takes that connection and allows you to build a relationship based on common ground.

No matter what demeanor you adopt, the key to success is making sure that everyone understands that you have shared concerns or interests. Are you at a loss as to how to do that in conversation? Try age. If you're a 45-year-old man, you probably have something in common with other 45-year-old men, even if it's just a backache. Having established that, you then move across that ground to the subject of your expertise.

Once you find common ground, you then use the reasons why one person might see another as an expert to move your audience toward acceptance of you in that role. One thing that makes this easier is knowing how to project acceptance through your body language. How all of this plays out, though, depends on your "script," that is, your strategy.

THE ROLE OF YOUR STRATEGY

Your choice of strategy affects how you establish rapport with people and how, ultimately, people will perceive you as an expert. Table 8-1 may help to root the different strategies in your mind.

In some cases, deciding which strategy is appropriate may be easy, just because of the kind of person you are. For example, Stone

Table 8-1.

Strategy	Summary	Type of Professional That You Might Link to It
Spider	Make point-to-point connections to link everything back to what you know	Politician or pundit (example: Jesse Jackson, who brings everything back to civil rights)
Stone Soup	You bring the recipe, and every-one else brings the ingredients	CEO, negotiator
Refiner	Turn overwhelming information into something usable	Public relations executive
Interpreter	Use understanding of special-ized language to build bridges	Project manager
Interrogator	Solve problems through data collection based on source leads	Management consultant
Pearl	Layer pertinent information on top of a kernel of facts	Journalist (example: legend-ary TV news journalist Ed Bradley)

Soup is natural for me because my fundamental expertise is human behavior. I know how to get people to contribute what they know to a meeting so that the whole is much greater than the sum of the parts.

It may not be so easy for you to choose a strategy if you're the executive assistant to the vice president of sales for your company and you have received orders to participate in strategic planning sessions. The president has decided that the company's five-year plan will benefit by having "everyone's" voice be heard, and you've been selected to be one of the 10 people in the 1,000-person company who will speak for "everyone." You see this as a big op-portunity to raise your profile and receive acknowledgment as a valuable member of the team, so you want to come across as an expert. You decide that the Interrogator strategy fits your goal best. Your primary challenge in that scenario is asking intelligent questions that drive people at the table toward problem solving. As part of your rapport building, and preparing people to see you in a different light through your strategy, you ask a question or two to get people thinking and talking about issues that are fundamental to corporate success, such as sales and cost-cutting measures. You don't have to have any answers; you just have to have good questions. Your bridge is that you are relying on your existing relationships with people to get cooperation.

As you continue to work down your chosen path, you will ultimately be successful when people accept you as an expert because of one of the reasons I covered in Chapter 1. In this early rapport-building stage, it's important to make sure that your strategy will actually get you there. Which of the following are you setting yourself up to achieve? Expertise because of:

- What you know that no one else does (isolation)

- Whom you know (affiliation)

- What you can do (demonstration)

- Your ability to make connections between ideas (association)

- Your skill in making sense of data, making it possible for people to use those data (generalization)

- Your perception of what's relevant, so that people care about something (humanizing)

- Your ability to relate data to what people already know, so that they're more inclined to contribute (adaptation)

- Your overwhelming knowledge or power, which gets people to shut up and listen (intimidation)

If you are the executive assistant at the meeting, this could play out in a number of ways, depending on your innate skill set. (Reminder: This is one of your background assets.) Whatever you do, just avoid what the "experts" do in the Holiday Inn Express ads: I may be only a clown at a child's birthday party, but I can help you ride the wild bull because I stayed at a Holiday Inn Express last night. You need to rely instead on the first part of the clown's approach in the ad: filling the head of your audience with your knowledge about the bull's bucking style and physical anomalies.

BODY LANGUAGE/RAPPORT

Your body language can directly reinforce one or more of the eight reasons for expertise, as I suggested in mentioning the ways you might position yourself at a table before a meeting starts. A companion piece is using body language to project the response you want from people. By relying on people's natural human inclination to mirror others as a way of assimilating, you subtly shift their mood by shifting their body language.

Moves to reinforce:

- Your use of illustrators and regulators will reinforce either a positive or a negative rapport with people in your audience. For example, you might baton with your arm if your aim is to intimidate, and you might nod generously if you want to encourage someone to continue contributing to the conversation.

- Avoid the use of barriers and adaptors, because they will make people feel shut out and uncomfortable. Even if you're the type who has a lot of nervous energy, find some way of controlling it: curl your toes; breathe rhythmically; mentally calculate how many people in the room would look better with Botox injections.

- Keep in mind the connection between mental processes and eye movement. I have told sales professionals that if they want to close a deal, they should put the pen and the contract to the right of the person. She then has to look down and to the right—the head position of deep emotion—as she thinks about signing. The down and to the left position is the calculating posture. Consider the circumstances, and where you are in the process of building rapport, before you drive someone's eyes one way or the other.

Moves to affect receptivity:

- You want to project appealing traits when people are teetering on the edge of accepting you, and you want to do so at a distance that is comfortable for the person. I want to offer a genuine smile and an open posture, while honoring the minimum of 18 inches of private space that people in the American culture expect. I am a large, imposing physical presence, so the last thing I want to do is get so close to someone that it unnerves her or makes him angry. On the other hand, a woman can often get away with coming closer to suggest a relationship of trust as she puts no barriers between her and another person and offers a genuine smile. Dropping barriers and smiling should evoke a mirroring on the part of the person(s) being addressed.

- Use your energy level to greatest advantage. Often, people will also mirror your energy level, as indicated by your pace of speech, illustrators, and posture. In establishing strong rapport, you may want to ramp up excitement by putting energy into your presentation, or you may decide that low energy serves you better. Why? If your strategy is to listen quietly and then come out with a zinger summation or observation, then you could end the session on a note that's much higher than any that were hit before in the meeting.

RUN YOUR APPROACH(ES)

Your implementation of strategy that begins with rapport building is in full swing in this phase of the process. This is where the techniques of persuasion come into play in a prominent way. I want to point out how different this phase is for an interrogator and for a person who wants acceptance as an expert. Your implementation has a level of complexity that interrogators do not have to build in.

In the interrogator's world, approaches are ploys. We use them to prey on people's motivations. If my role in the interrogation is to have the source see me as a friend, then my approach helps push him toward believing I'm his friend. If my source is a colonel and my goal is to come across as his equal, then I choose approaches to reinforce that perception.

The skills you are learning here are much more comprehensive, even though they involve the same principles. To gain acceptance as an expert, you have to do more than stroke someone's ego or trade cigarettes for weapons information. It is much easier to take a prisoner who is under duress and psychologically prod and poke him—that is, use approaches—to set yourself up as an expert and extract information. To achieve your desired outcome of convincing normal people in normal situations that you are an expert, you must build a strategy that is reinforced by something comparable to approaches, that is, what I've referred to as *techniques*.

APPROACHES, AKA TECHNIQUES

On the left of Table 8-2 are the names of some of the main approaches that interrogators use, as well as the basic definitions. On the right are the comparable techniques.

Table 8-2.

Approach	Interrogator Meaning	Technique
Direct	Asking straightforward questions	Direct questioning
Incentive	Quid pro quo: I show you mine, you show me yours; or, more commonly, I give you something you need, such as food, and you give me some data	Offering incentives
Emotional	Focused on "love of" or "hate of," such as love of country or hatred of your dictator	Playing on emotions
Fear up (harsh or mild)	Preying on what the source has to lose	Criticism
Pride-and-ego (up or down)	Flattery can get you everywhere, but with some sources, taking them down a notch reminds them how worthless they are relative to you	Flattery (up)
Futility	No matter what, you will not get what you want . . . unless you work with me on this	Futility
We know all	I am the expert; I know more than you do	Omniscience
Repetition	Driving home the point repeatedly, not necessarily by saying the same thing; maybe I just don't understand	Ignorance, or naïveté
Silence	Leveraging the fact that most human beings hate silence; a way to get control because people say all kinds of things to fill the air	Silence

Many of these techniques readily support the strategy you've chosen. So while I as an interrogator would use them overtly as motivators, you as the expert will use them subtly to direct attention where you want it, affect mood, and reinforce key messages. Consider how you would use a few of these techniques if your strategy were the Spider. You find the conversation moving toward medical issues and away from your area of expertise, nutrition, so you ask a direct question: "Did she rely on any special dietary regimen after that surgery?" You could also take an emotional approach: "You could help your wife heal faster after that surgery just by adding a few simple nutrients to her meals." Or use the technique of omniscience: "I've had that surgery, and my doctor said I healed twice as fast as most patients because of my diet." In each case, the conversation loops back to your area without your sounding like the Vanderbilt lady.

QUESTION

The questioning phase of interrogation is where we pay the bills as an interrogator. All of my research, establishing control, and establishing rapport, as well as my approaches, are geared to one thing: getting information. I get it by asking questions.

This phase is about achieving your desired outcome. You start to extract information, all the while remembering control, rapport, and the approach or strategy you are presenting.

In an interrogation, while I am asking questions, I must constantly reinforce that I am the source's friend, or I'm there to help, or I'm his worst nightmare. You will do the same thing to achieve your desired outcome. With your strategies and techniques, you constantly reinforce the idea that you are an expert and you are using tools to do it. Unlike an interrogator, you are not trying to extract information, you are extracting acceptance.

As an interrogator, I take into account which kinds of questions affect my source's mind and what their effect is likely to be. I attempt to extract information from the source's mind in ways that are consistent with how he stored the information so that I can get it quickly. For example, if he tends to pin things to time, then I ask questions in terms of, "When did that happen?" You will need to do the same. Good, bad, or ugly, questions can absolutely affect your rapport and your image.

Despite the contrasting objectives—my wanting to extract information; your wanting to extract acceptance—questions play a major role in pursuing both. In some cases, the type of questions you use to establish expertise will be just like those that interrogators use to extract information. The categories of questions are:

- **Control.** This is a question that you know the answer to. You use it to establish a baseline, but you can also use it with a loud guy, for example, to find out how much information he really does have about your area of expertise. You can also use it to give you time to think. As you ask a question and let someone else have the floor, she reinforces your expertise.

- **Direct.** This type of question speaks for itself: Just ask. In this case, you should be aware that a solid question that elicits a narrative response needs to be well structured or you may get a vague or rambling answer ("What single thing did you find most frightening about camping in the desert for two weeks?"). Asking a question that sets someone up to digress can undermine you and be counterproductive to the discussion ("What kind of scary things did you see out there in the desert?"). If the person does start to ramble, you can save yourself by allowing him to talk until your point is made and then cutting him short. The benefit is invaluable, but you have to do it skillfully so that he doesn't feel as though you cut him off in mid-sentence.

- **Repeat.** You asked the question before, but you now ask it again in a different form because you didn't learn what you needed to learn. A shift in body language and a change in word choice will let you pull it off. This technique can be used as a pause to allow you time to think or even to loop data back to an anchor point and allow you to move back onto one of the strands of your web. It is used best when you ask a parallel question that causes someone to bring up the earlier subject and reinforce your position.

- **Leading.** Journalists with an agenda do this all the time. In quizzing a disgraced senator who denies any wrongdoing, the question might be, "When you gambled on that baseball game, did you care that it was illegal?" The question leads listeners into concluding that the senator did, in fact, gamble on the baseball game.

- **Compound.** Use this only if you want to confuse someone: "Did you want to deliver that presentation after lunch or go to Janie's birthday party in the employee lounge?"

- **Canned.** These are prepackaged questions, like those you would build out of Wikipedia descriptions. They can make you sound well informed if you insert them at the right time, but you have to know enough about the subject matter to know when they are misplaced. If someone is talking about the World Series, it's probably a bit jarring for you to ask a question about sabermetrics—unless you can apply it to the discussion at hand. Canned questions allow the interrogator to build the framework of her interrogation so that if anything gets too far off the path, she can use a canned question to double back and ensure that she got all the details. Canned questions can also allow an interrogator to get the structure of the question right in terms of very complex subject matter. Most litigators use this approach to questioning.

Hopefully, all kinds of applications of these questions jump into your mind. Repeat questions could help you use the Refiner or the Pearl. Direct questions will make Stone Soup work. With the Spider, you might use canned questions to keep people on subjects you know, or leading questions to direct people to the conclusion you want to emphasize or to get them to reinforce your ideas so that others make that connection.

The most powerful question is the one that your audience can't answer—but you can. Or at least the members of your audience think you can. When you leave your audience with a tough question of your design, then you are forever the expert. Perhaps they can't wait to see you again so that you can answer it. Or maybe you'll never see them again, but the last thing they remember about you is that you made them think. Either way, you're an expert.

CASE STUDIES

I took a single, real scenario and approached it from two ways to give you a sense of how strategies supported by techniques and questions can help a wannabe expert deliver the goods.

Scenario summary: A severe drought causes a governor to ask the president to declare a state of emergency in nearly half the counties in his state. He also wants permission to override agreements with neighboring jurisdictions that affect their water supply. (Important note: The scenario summary is true; however, the process of exploring it contains speculation about how different people would react.)

USE OF THE PEARL IN A ONE-ON-ONE

A junior investigative reporter has the assignment to get to the governor in the next two hours and interview him. Her aim is to get him to reveal his plans and to make specific statements about what those plans will mean to the average person in the state. Here is how the encounter might play out.

- The reporter goes into the interview knowing the information given in the scenario and one set of facts that's relevant—the nub of the Pearl: The state has an inflated housing market, with 1 in 299 people having lost a home during the rash of foreclosures in 2007. Many people are living in more house than they can afford. A small squeeze to their financial position, and they will join the swelling numbers of people who have lost their homes.

- The reporter confronts the governor about an emotional issue: his concern that average citizens will get rid of him in the next election if they don't have water.
  - The technique plays on "love of"—in this case, "love of power."

- The reporter does not have to know anything deep about the issue at that point to ask the question: "How has that concern affected your judgment about the economic impact of overriding the agreement with neighboring states?"
  - This is a leading question that implies that the governor's personal priorities are more important to him than the welfare of the citizenry.

- A denial brings an explanation that the economic welfare of the state has been considered.
  - A politician in this spot is likely to try to pull a preemptive strike. If the state is known for its golf courses and cheap electric power, then he'll probably try to reassure you that those elements of the economy will remain strong.
  - If he doesn't offer anything other than a denial, then silence could be an effective technique. Silence from a reporter implies, "You owe me more, and you know it."

- "So what you're doing won't have any effect on things like water for golf courses and hydroelectric power?" she asks after she learns about them in his protracted denial.

  ○ Layer on layer, she's building the Pearl. Going into the session, she didn't know about the importance of these things.

- He offers another denial: That's not what I meant. There will be an impact, he concedes. But he's taking steps to mitigate it.

  ○ The more emotional he gets, the less cognitive he is. Asking questions that create the need for one denial after another will probably get him to leak more information than he'd intended.

  ○ She watches his body language and sees adaptors. "This line of questioning is really getting to him," she concludes.

  ○ Now she pulls out a canned question that a colleague had given her as she walked out the door. It hadn't made any sense to her before now, but she suddenly sees why it has relevance: "You are aware that the water release you propose to curtail is the water that drives hydroelectric production for peak hours in facilities in the southern part of the state, aren't you?" Not being stupid, the governor won't simply say no. Saying yes, however, means that he must follow with facts of some kind that don't make him look careless. More ammo for her.

- When she asks him about the specific steps he is taking to address the potential impact on hydroelectric power, she has backed him into a corner. Now, she reigns as an expert because his response will open the door to myriad questions related to economic impact on business, on homeowners who can barely afford to pay their mortgages, and on trade relationships with other states.

USE OF STONE SOUP IN A TOWN MEETING

A city councilman goes to a town meeting with the governor and is mad as heck about the water situation in his state, and particularly his city. He'd like nothing more than to disgrace the governor so that he never gets elected again. Here is how the encounter might play out.

- The city councilman sees that the governor is flanked by an economist, a housing expert, and the administration's top environmental guy. Immediately, he figures that the little bit he knows about the situation is his "magic stone."

- His opening volley isn't even a question. He says to the environmental expert: "I have some serious doubts about your environmental impact statements related to this issue."

  - This is criticism designed to get someone to spill information about what he's done. In this case, the councilman seizes the opportunity to talk about something that the governor doesn't even know about: a series of source water assessment reports done for the counties in the state.

- A reporter takes over, saying that she saw those reports, and the one for the capital city had no substance at all. She holds it up and asks why it's only three pages long, while the one for a really small county up north has a thorough, 16-page analysis.

  - The first vegetable goes into the soup. By citing an official document that shows poor planning, the reporter flavors the soup exactly as the city councilman had hoped.

- A farmer asks what he's supposed to do when the government takes away the water he needs for his crops, which help to feed people and livestock in many different states.

  - If the governor and his economist sidekick do not have a plan that they can recite in response to, "What am I supposed to do?" then they do not have a good answer. The soup is coming together.

- The city councilman turns to the woman next to him and whispers, "Why do they have that housing guy up there? Is this going to create problems for homeowners?" That causes her to jump to her feet with a flurry of accusations that the governor's actions will raise the cost of power in the state by 40 percent, making it impossible for many people to afford both their mortgages and their electricity.

  - More and more elements are coming together because the city councilman's recipe for condemnation is made real by the contributions of people that he energized with a simple observation and some follow-up comments.

When the city councilman gets back to his hometown, he can say, "I built a coalition of truth to uncover the real facts in this situation." Each of the soup contributors will remember the flavor of his own ingredient best, and maybe even think that the recipe turned out all wrong, but regardless of that, the soup has been made. In this case, the city councilman is insulated. Any negative publicity attacks not just him, but also the greater group and gives him more renown.

I could give you ways in which this same scenario could yield different outcomes for people using multiple strategies, techniques, packaging styles, and questions, but it's your job to play with those variables now.

Exercise: Design Success

Take the same scenario, or use any current story from the news media, and create outcomes that you design by using the elements I described here. First, get a clear picture in your mind of the hypothetical situation you will face—a one-on-one, a small meeting, a large meeting, and so on—and then go through the process of establishing control and rapport, using techniques to support your strategy, and driving toward your outcome with questions.

In an interrogation, I may establish expertise, but only as much as I need to extract the information I need. Prisoners are in a different psychological state from your audiences, but they still need to be convinced that I am what I say I am; otherwise their motivation to talk to me evaporates. As you try to gain acceptance as an expert, you need to keep talking long enough to get what you want, but you also need to know when to stop. Use your strategy and supporting tools to ensure that the audience stays with you, get its buy-in, and then move on. In an interrogation, we know that the conversation will flow to a point where termination should occur. Next, I'll look at how you will do that in your role as expert.

CHAPTER

9

KNOWING WHEN TO STOP

¤ ¤ ¤

A play begins with an inciting incident and ends when the protagonist stops changing. You can argue with that definition, but the point is that the curtain does not come down at an arbitrary point; the play is not over simply because people stop talking, nor should it continue after the story is over. In other words, part of presenting your expertise effectively is managing the termination of the session.

As long as your storyline reflects reasonable expectations for wowing the audience, you get to determine the beginning and end of your play. On the other hand, if your reason for buying this book is that you're a motivational speaker who has sold yourself as a cold fusion lecturer for an eight-hour session, then all I can say is that the end is nearer than you want it to be.

So, keep your expected outcome in mind, as well as the limits of your abilities. If you used a strategy like Stone Soup to solve a software problem—hear the applause coming from all departments!—do not fall so in love with the reflection of an expert that you now see in the mirror that you feel the need to solve world hunger. Understand the scope of your desired outcome, and know when it is enough. In plain English, know when and how to shut up.

THE CONCEPT OF TERMINATION

Termination is not the same as simply shutting up; it's driven by the aim of achieving a controlled exit.

Interrogators may terminate a session for any of a number of reasons:

1. They are out of time.

2. The source is out of information, at least for the time being.

3. They are out of plan; that is, they realize that they have to regroup. Interrogators go into a session with a grand plan that changes the minute we talk to the source. All of the planning we've spent our time on does not take the human dynamic into account. Sometimes a prisoner brings up something he has done that is beyond an interrogator's capacity to hear. That conversation needs a different questioner. Or maybe the interrogator just cannot find the right approach or words to persuade the prisoner to talk. Termination is a way to make the transition to a colleague without losing continuity. This is the opposite of establishing control; it is about maintaining and reinforcing control to enable a productive exit.

4. The approach the interrogators are taking includes a midstream termination. I go in as the heavy and act harshly; right behind me, someone much friendlier comes in to "rescue" the source. (Let me remind you that this is all "theater for one." No source I have ever interrogated was ever in any physical danger from me or my colleagues.) I may remain in the room as the heavy, or I may leave. I need to ensure that I can pull off either action.

HOW INTERROGATORS TERMINATE

One of the biggest differences between an amateur and a professional interrogator is the effective termination.

Regardless of where we are in the process, a termination is more than simply saying, "That's it," and walking out. Getting into the situation required control, rapport, and strategy; getting out of the situation reverses the process.

Good interrogators first emphasize the control issue, and whatever rapport they have managed to build. In the case of the bad cop, this may be nothing more than saying to the source, "You had better hope I never see you again," and storming out. Most of the time, however, it involves reinforcing the approach that got the prisoner to talk. In your terms, this means emphasizing the rapport and driving home the strategy that worked. Interrogators also have to remember the reason they were in the room to start with—weapons information, troop strength, and so on. As they do this, they revisit the plan. They wrap up what they have talked about and remind the source that others of their kind will probably be talking to him later. Interrogators often send the prisoner back to his cell to try to recall more details—a kind of POW homework, if you will. This allows them to break the interrogation into manageable sessions so that they can go off and complete their reports in a timely fashion.

Planning enables you to compartmentalize information and recap key facts. It also reminds you of the structure that you put in place and allows you natural break points. If you are close to the time you anticipated ending the session, then you can put the facts in order and wrap up in a meaningful way. If you had planned objectives that were not met, you can create a synopsis and point to the next session.

Interrogators do not necessarily script an end to a session; we have to respect the fluid nature of the encounter. When pertinent data come out of a session, we do not want to yell, "Gee, thanks!" and rush out of the room to report it. That is a sure recipe for letting your source know what is important to you, and a great way to make him go silent.

Many professionals who are experts in their fields know this lesson. For example, the vice president of human resources is invited to attend the CEO's quarterly meeting. He is there to discuss attrition and new hires. The meeting also includes operations and finance experts, who are there to discuss their areas as well. The human resources vice president speaks first about exit interviews and the results pointing to employee satisfaction. The CEO is pleased to learn causes and mitigation. The HR VP then finishes on a high note and sits quietly and listens while the other two brief the CEO on their respective issues. He comments only when the topic of conversation relates directly to his area. This is the most difficult of lessons for most people to learn. It is better to be quiet and be assumed to be ignorant than to open your mouth and remove all doubt.

You would terminate a session for the same reasons interrogators do, and I'll explore that later in this chapter. But for now, I will point out what not to do.

REMOVING ALL DOUBT

Terminating a session because you are out of time might be a result of poor planning, or it might be part of a planning success. It's poor planning if you've miscalculated how long you needed to present your expertise. It's a win if you got your audience so involved that you ran out of time long before you ran out of information. What you don't want to do is convey the impression you've been caught off guard. Statements like, "Oops. That's all I've got unless you've got something else" are a setup for disaster.

Running out of information too soon, of course, is not where you want to be. If that happens, remember three rules:

1. Do not keep talking just to fill the air. The phrase (a Gumpism) "That's all I have to say about that" can serve you much better because it leaves the impression that you could offer other thoughts if you chose to.

2. Do not make stuff up or suddenly go wildly off track in the conversation. If you've run out of things to say about Nobel laureates, you would be unwise to suggest that Joe Theismann should be the first person to win both the Heisman Trophy and a Nobel Peace Prize.

3. Do not make a confrontational remark to distract from your lack of additional facts. The absolute worst time to make a comment like that is when you're out of information. Even if you can back it up with the facts you've already stated, you're still invalidated. Merely repeating what has become old information will not help you save face or win the argument.

For people who have enjoyed acceptance as an expert, the temptation to pontificate about something off topic can be intense. They run out of information about topic A—no problem. They just move on to topic B. Your ego should never be the driver behind the staging of a termination. That has to be intellect, not ego. The thing that will quickly kill acceptance of you as an expert is a need to expound on everything once you've scored in one area. Consider the strange case of Dr. James Watson. Watson, a discoverer of the DNA double helix, should have stuck with genetics instead of saying to a British newspaper that testing showed that blacks are intellectually inferior. That blew up in his face on October 18, 2007. A day later, he apologized and said that his remark had been misinterpreted. (You've heard the expression "A day late and a dollar short?") All of a sudden, the fact that he'd won the Nobel Prize for Science in 1962 seemed like nothing more than a piece of ancient history that allowed him to mouth off about the future of Africa. The balloon marked "expert" that had followed him around everywhere he went for 45 years started losing air. The British government's skills minister, David Lammy, summed up what many people were thinking: "It is a shame that a man with a record of scientific distinction should see his work overshadowed by his own irrational prejudices" (CNN, October 19, 2007).

Regarding being "out of plan," just like an interrogator who is meeting a source for the first time, you can find yourself surprised by your audience's lack of response or negative response to your strategy. Don't persist with something that's failing. If you're not getting through the way you want to, then it's time for a new plan. The way you will know that is by observing body language. If you can remember to capitalize on your gains and consolidate them, you will terminate correctly. Knowing that I have gained some credibility in a field where I had none is validation enough for me; I choose to leave while I can. Remember, it is seldom necessary to be the most knowledgeable person alive. You probably have not sold yourself as a guest speaker on cold fusion and then picked up this book to get ready. Being expert is about being expert enough and then terminating while you still are. Know when to shut up.

MOVES THAT SIGNAL TERMINATION

In an interrogation, there are a few indicators that the end is near: The source stops talking. He says he doesn't know any more. He falls asleep. You fall asleep.

When you are taking the role of expert, body language will tell you when people are starting to disbelieve you, which is one reason to move on, and it will indicate when you've made them uncomfortable, perhaps because they feel sorry for you. It will also tell you when everyone is solidly in your camp, at which point you want to find a reason to cut your presentation short because you've won. Don't be the actor who does a schlock horror film right after winning an Oscar. Oh, and by the way, if the audience falls asleep, you have gone on too long. Right now, go back to that chart in Chapter 3 and revisit the body language that signals disbelief, discomfort, and total acceptance. This gives you the strongest indicators of whether the audience wants you to stay or go.

When you hit the crossroads, then what? If the body language you see indicates uncertainty, or a mixed bag of believers and nonbelievers, you have to decide if you have enough information left to repackage it and approach the challenge in a different way. Think hard, and look at those faces. Have you generally achieved your goal, with only a few people being unwilling to give you a standing ovation? If so, leave on a high note. If the uncertainty dominates, though, draw from the upcoming "how to" on termination.

REVISITING THE PLANNING ELEMENTS

In order to handle a termination well, particularly if it involves repackaging information or adopting a new strategy in mid-presentation, you need to have your audience, duration, and desired outcome in mind. At this stage of the game, you will approach them from a different angle, however. You need to ask yourself "rescue questions": Did I misjudge who I'd be talking to, and if so, how? Did I miscalculate the time I have to pull this off? Where am I on the path to achieving my outcome—still at the beginning, or somewhere along the way?

AUDIENCE

Audience is everything. That same CNN piece that quoted David Lammy about Dr. James Watson's faux pas noted that during a lecture tour in 2000, Watson had previously "suggested there might be links between a person's weight and their level of ambition and between skin color and sexual prowess." If Jon Stewart said the former on *The Daily Show* and Chris Rock said the latter in an HBO special, people would laugh, not wave the banner of political incorrectness. Why? Audience. In both cases, the audiences expect irreverence. But no one goes to a lecture by the eminent Dr. Watson and expects it—even though he followed up his sexual prowess comment with a joke: "You never heard of an English lover. Only an English patient."

The whole issue of trying to connect with your audience by being witty is fraught with complications. What you think is witty is going to be offensive to somebody; are you really sure that that somebody is not in the room? Conservative pundit Ann Coulter can get a laugh from Sean Hannity on his Fox TV show when she makes fun of some "godless" Democrat, but if she says the same thing to Matt Lauer on the *Today Show*, who's laughing?

Why don't people just get over "it" and laugh?

- Part of not laughing is not liking the person—what you are saying at the moment may be funny, but you don't have a history of amusing me. This is the plight of Ann Coulter, humorist.

- When people are stressed, they don't have a sense of humor. After the *Achille Lauro* hijacking in 1985, a comedian at an open mic night in Washington, DC, made a joke about the incident. Structurally, it was funny, but the timing was all wrong. Nothing the comedian said after that could get the audience on his side again.

So do not try to win over your audience or, even worse, save yourself from having aroused people's anger by making a joke. Unless you know your audience extremely well, in which case you will probably be forgiven for an offensive remark, you cannot predict the sense of humor of every person who is listening to you. I briefly worked for a colonel who called jokes CEOs—career-ending opportunities.

Not all people will connect with your style, of course, and in some cases the situation and presentation are a gross mismatch (like the *Achille Lauro* joke mentioned earlier). In other cases, your audience is just not receptive to the message. Cut your losses. Regroup if you see that mismatch filling the air with tension. Knowing that not all people will be receptive to new ideas does more to show that you are expert than trying to do CPR on a dead horse. Remember that expertise is about information intersecting with people. If there's no intersection, there's no expertise.

DURATION

Interrogators know that most soldiers have a maximum of 48 hours of vulnerability. If your unit notices that you're missing, whatever intelligence you have about firepower, positions, and plans will change within that time, so that your information becomes stale rapidly. The lesson for you in this is to hold on to facts as long as you can, avoiding blurting out every last thing you know up front. By doing that, even if you find that you have miscalculated how long you have to present your expertise, you can choose the correct tactic to close:

- You've run out of time, so you barrage your audience with a stunning array of facts, like the finale of a fireworks display.

- You have one great fact left, so you take your parting shot like a sniper.

- You have a few relevant, but not momentous, facts left, so you end with a repartee (fire/counterfire).

The tale of Rumpelstiltskin offers some good guidance. After helping the miller's daughter spin straw into gold so that she could impress the king, the dwarf came to claim his prize: her firstborn son. She pleaded and cried—this doesn't work with interrogators, by the way—and the dwarf finally said, "You can keep the kid if you can guess my name." Her delaying tactics enabled her to discover his name and be rid of him forever.

You can pull off this time-delay move if you have established some degree of deference. Keep the conversation going long enough to conclude with a profound statement—and then leave. The last one to amaze the audience is the smartest person in the room. Stay on topic, though. Do not try to trump the next guy just to get the last big idea into the air.

OUTCOME

Are you sure you didn't change outcomes in the middle of the presentation? Did you start off wanting simply to gain acceptance as a knowledgeable person, and then find yourself focused on impressing the gorgeous blonde?

Just like Dr. Watson, you can become enamored with your hard-won image when it starts to yield perks for you. If your original outcome was to carry on an intelligent conversation with your new boss, and you find yourself trying instead to seduce the boss's new assistant with your prowess in a meeting, then you have gone awry. Go back to your plan.

On the other hand, sometimes you do need to change outcomes. An interrogator who finds that his source is the general's driver, and that his preparation was inadequate for a session with that source, needs to revisit his intended outcomes. In a situation like that, all you can get from the initial encounter is an understanding of the magnitude of the problem. The interrogator would have to find out which general this guy worked for, how long he worked for the general, and whether or not he has any motivation to talk. Without additional time for research, the option is to restart the process: Establish control and rapport, rely on a strategy that seems appropriate for him, and then terminate without delving deeply into the subject matter. The hoped-for result at that point is another meeting at another time.

If you go into a meeting with a well-prepared discussion of baseball, only to find out that the person's real passion is not the game in general, but specifically left-handed pitchers who had an ERA under 1.5, then you will be poorly prepared to be the expert. You will have two options: Change the direction of the conversation to one of "I am just starting to learn about baseball, and I cannot imagine how long it took to get your kind of knowledge . . . where did you start?" or terminate and go back to the drawing board. Either is fine, based on personalities—yours and his. Keep reminding yourself that expertise is about information meeting people.

With poise and confidence (stand up straight), you can let the person know in a straightforward way that you have *some* knowledge of her area of expertise and that you value her insights. This is an opportunity to reinforce the strategy that you will use.

In the case of the general's driver, I might start my strategy by offering him an incentive, and stroke his ego as to his importance as I say, "You must be very trustworthy to hold this position." And then I leave him alone to smoke a couple of cigarettes as I spend 20 minutes regrouping at the situation tent.

This basic decision of whether to terminate or to redirect is crucial, because it can mean the difference between coming across as being an expert and being an idiot.

HANDLING A TERMINATION

There is no hard rule for how to terminate, whether you are dealing with an interrogation or a business meeting. You need to rely on your own background assets, as well as the skill-specific tools that you learned from the chapters in Part 2.

The purpose of termination, whether you are going to leave the room or leave the conversation yet stay present, is the same. You bridge your expertise back to who you are and who you have become in the session.

Once he's voiced the brilliant idea of putting all invoices online, which will change the bottom line for his company, "Bob the mailroom guy" is only part of the person's identity. After presenting his idea, he will probably terminate his portion of the session, sitting quietly as people talk about aspects of the issue until the finance guys validate his idea by looking at the magnitude of the mailings per month. This kind of termination leaves the expert fully in the conversation, but the key is to resist the temptation to ramble while you're still sitting there.

Once you've won, sit there and bask in the validation.

USE OF TACTICS

Finish your remarks with a tactic that matches the kind of information you have left. Returning to the example of James Watson, once he was attacked in the media for making his statement about the intelligence of blacks, he could do only two of three things, depending on his information and convictions:

1. Come back with dominant scientific evidence that his statement had legitimacy (if his assertion were fact instead of his opinion). He might cite studies in neurobiology, genetics, and other relevant disciplines to reinforce what he had said. Tactic: Barraging, or the use of overwhelming force.

2. Say nothing at first. Wait until one of his critics who is black, such as David Lammy, makes a stupendous error in judgment, then, on the same day, apologize for his remark about blacks. Tactic: Sniper, or taking a shot when the target is most vulnerable.

3. Assert again and again that he was misquoted, misrepresented, and misunderstood. Tactic: Counterfire, or returning fire to protect himself.

Watson chose number three and, in military terms, counterfired in retrograde, meaning that he returned fire as he was backing up. A quick apology bought him some time to rethink his statement and retarget. He came back with a stronger denial about "no scientific basis" for such a statement.

What you need to know if you want to sustain your reputation as an expert is this: If you're going to open your mouth and say something that may inflame people's sensibilities, you'd better have enough facts to back it up—enough facts to intimidate people into recognizing the legitimacy of your statement. Otherwise, you have no substantial tactical options.

SWITCHING STRATEGIES

An effective termination move when you have hit the wall is to switch strategies so that another expert can jump in with new information. For example, you can do this by directing all your attention toward a problem and asking questions to drive toward the solution (Interrogator), eliciting contributions from everyone in a workshop model (Stone Soup), or getting your audience to lay more layers of knowledge on what you have (the Pearl).

Let's say I talk baseball with a baseball fanatic and throw around enough facts to sound like a fan. He feels confident that I'm knowledgeable, so he lets loose with the jargon, and I think he's speaking a foreign language. I prey on human drives, and I say, "I have really gotten into baseball because I woke up and realized it's a great part of life that I've missed, but I'm still new to the game." That's likely to evoke a response like, "You sure know more than most people who just got into it. You must like it as much as I do!" At that point, he'll feel as though I recognize his expertise, and he'll jump into the role of mentor to bring me up a few notches. That's the Pearl.

PLANT A QUESTION

Earlier in this chapter, I referred to "POW homework." You can effect a termination with homework, too.

When I teach body language, I deliberately plant very difficult concepts at the end of the class. This makes the folks who hired me want to bring me back if it's a one-day class. If it's a two-day class, then my action creates mailboxes in everyone's head so that they have a place to put the things we'll talk about the next day. Then they come into the class with questions, full of ideas, and ready for an epiphany. When they get the answers, I'm the guru who showed them the light, the one they will always connect with body language expertise.

Even if you know you will never see your audience again, its members will remember you with regard if the last thing out of your mouth is a provocative question.

How will you use this information next?

10

RESCUE SCHEMES

¤ ¤ ¤

One of the most awkward feelings I've ever had was during a production of Ayn Rand's *The Night of January 16*, which is set entirely in a courtroom. I played a gangster named Guts Regan, who had lots and lots of lines. As all courtroom dramas do, the story played out through examination and cross-examination, so most of my cues were lines like, "And then what?" and "What was next?" There was no reference point for me in case I forgot a line, and no logical opportunity for someone to start talking, either to give me time to think or to feed me information that would trigger my memory. With no theatrical lighting and no distinctive stage movement, there wasn't even a technical cue that I might get from what was going on around me. Add to the lack of anchor points the fact that the audience was 10 feet away. I could see every one of their faces, and they could see every drop of sweat on mine.

I hit a moment where I could not remember where I had been or where I had to go. My fellow cast members sat around me; one stood right in front of my face. All of them were staring hopefully, unable to throw out a line to help. I looked up at the clock on the wall and watched the second hand tick, tick, tick. How many seconds does it take to drown?

What to do?

- Swim to safety?

- Call for help?

- Stand on someone else's shoulders so that I could breathe while he drowned?

Yes, I saved myself. I have buried the dramatic conclusion of my trauma somewhere in this chapter.

A lapse of memory is one of many reasons why you might need a rescue scheme, and poor planning and preparation are not the cause of many of these lapses. For example, your meeting might go much longer than anyone had planned. You've sold yourself well, and now you're in the crosshairs—with no more material. Or an unexpected person might join the audience after you have succeeded in winning over his colleagues; he's a contrarian, and so your progress screeches to a halt as everyone hears him challenge you.

Regardless of the reason for the problem, the ways out fall into three categories: saving yourself, engaging someone else in helping you, and building yourself up by making someone else look bad. (Don't cringe at the last one. If someone goes for your jugular vein, you can either make him stop or bleed to death. Machiavellian tactics have a place in life; you just don't want them to drive everything you do.)

In preparation for learning the specifics of rescuing yourself, here are a few general guidelines that apply across the board:

- **Remain composed.** You are the expert; maintain the body language of confidence. If necessary, leave the room for a moment, or stride over to the water pitcher to give yourself a breather. (Note: I have had to do this recently, so don't think for a minute that only the timid or inexperienced face the challenge of remaining composed.)

- **Always have a contingency plan.** As Foghorn Leghorn said, "Fortunately, I keep my feathers numbered for just such an emergency."

In each of the following sections, I offer you specifics on useful body language and the kinds of plans you need if you are to pull off a particular rescue scheme. Right now, I want you to focus on the absolute necessity of including contingency plans in your preparation to become an expert. Remember: If you're prepared for your adventure, the answer you need in a crisis will come.

Take a lesson from extreme athletes, who have to develop the skill of effectively evaluating their options because they have a different way of looking at the world. Where other people see only danger, they see fun. The only way they can take that approach and still survive time after time is with contingency planning that matches the kind that soldiers use. This means drilling until the subroutines are locked in your head, so that on the occasions when something goes wrong, you waste no energy on panicking. You simply invest energy in solving the problem because the solutions have become second nature.

Maryann's ocean whitewater kayaking instructors taught her that their years of experience in isolated surf zones, complex rock gardens, and dark sea caves didn't reduce their risk one bit; however, those years did give them more practice in thinking through options when the unexpected happens. One day, this happened in a big way. A 15-foot-high rogue wave hit Maryann's friend Eric while he was paddling near rock reefs; he was trapped. The day before the incident, though, Eric and his teammate Jim had speculated about what they would do if they knew that a wave would slam them against the rocks. Jim's river kayaking background told him to lean toward the obstacle to avoid being pinned against it. He reconsidered. No, he concluded, the ocean withdraws after the wave, so you won't get pinned. The greater danger is having your body smashed into the cliff. Lean into the wave; go hull-first into the rocks. That's what Eric did when the rogue wave hit him, and it saved his life.

You will have to think through contingencies in the same manner because some of the solutions to your being trapped will be as counterintuitive as this one. Eric learned to avoid the trap of doing "what comes naturally." It saved his life. If you do what your gut tells you, you could drown.

SWIM TO SAFETY

If you're going to swim to safety, you have to know how to swim.

Polished presenters have routines that they rely on when hecklers take them off course, the projector crashes, or any number of other disruptions occur. They include self-deprecating humor and agilely moving to another topic, among other things. Seasoned professors have their own version of this: They tell a story with a memorable lesson or throw out a question that keeps students pondering the answer for a week.

In order to save yourself, you can use verbal and body language maneuvers to effect smooth transitions, either to a termination or to a new phase of your presentation. Here are your basic options.

VERBAL

- **Change the subject.** Regardless of what strategy you've been relying on, you can use a Spider-like maneuver to move off the topic that's causing you to fumble and onto a topic you can handle. Without sounding like the lady with Alzheimer's who brought everything back to Vanderbilt, you want to move deftly to a new subject. Put the Kevin Bacon game you did in Chapter 5 in full play.

- **Condition the question.** This is an evasive maneuver that's designed to let you give an answer that's true, but that does not answer the actual question. It buys time and, if it's done well, shifts the conversation into less threatening territory. Listen to celebrities of any kind in tough interviews and you hear them conditioning questions. The most famous example is probably President Bill Clinton's response when asked a straightforward question about his relationship with Monica Lewinsky. Instead of giving the requested "yes" or "no," he said, "I did not have sexual relations with that woman."

- **Tell a related story or supply a little-known fact.** Your information on alternative fuels is down to a trickle, so you mention that the United Nations expert on the right to food thinks that increased biofuel production has had catastrophic effects on the world's hungry because it's disrupting their food supply. (He did say that, by the way.) The discussion is likely to take on an emotionally charged tone involving battling views on political correctness, and you are off the hook for a while. Do not get sucked into the discussion. Instead, use this brief respite to get your feet back under you.

- **Terminate the meeting.** As I noted in the last chapter, "I'm not prepared to go any further today" can help you hang on to the success you've already scored without casting any shadows on your performance.

- **Inject self-deprecating humor.** Giving people permission to laugh at you is a pressure-release tactic. People do it all the time by citing "blonde moments" or "senior moments." However, you should use this technique only if you can carry it off and if it's consistent with the way you've presented your expertise. If you have set yourself up as an Interpreter or a Refiner, for example, this may not work. In both cases, people have been looking to you to help them connect with some arcane vocabulary or concepts, so throwing in a joke about your competence could undermine your entire strategy.

- **Recap.** Find a different way to revisit your key points. If you had slides with bullets, then try to talk about the material graphically: "You could stack these facts in a pyramid, with the top one being . . ." Or if you had been talking through material in a narrative form, then summarize it in bullet form. Another way to go is to recap with the focus on a conclusion: "We started this whole conversation with A. I think it comes to a resolution with F, but maybe we should all run down A through E to see if that makes sense." This might give you just enough time for your white matter to make the connections that will shape a powerful concluding statement. If this does not work, you could always use the age-old "give the prisoners some homework" ploy of the interrogator that I described in Chapter 9. Do this with something like, "We have gotten from A to E today with a lot of brainstorming and hard work. I think we should take 24 hours to evaluate the validity of these steps before concluding our decision. A sort of sanity check. Let's sleep on it and plan on a brief conversation in the morning."

- **Close with a bang.** This is the Dirty Harry approach. Clint squints at the dirtball in the movies and says, "In all the confusion, I forgot. Did I fire five rounds or six? No, you have to ask yourself, do I feel lucky? Well, do ya?" If you frag one guy, the next one is not likely to step up. This preys on human uncertainty by inviting people to take a chance when the odds are stacked against them. In your situation, it means that you have a significant piece of information that you can pull out when the odds are stacking up against you. You use it, and then move to, "That's all for now."

- **Say something game-changing.** This is one way to start the discussion all over. Going back to the U.N. expert's comment on biofuel, you can reframe an entire discussion of alternative fuels to give yourself a plethora of new opportunities by citing an expert like that and saying, "Frankly, until I read that yesterday, I had not considered that kind of implication of biofuel production. I'm still internally debating that one— what do you think?"

- **Add a show stopper.** This doesn't even have to be information about the subject area, as long as it is tangentially related to what was just said. It can be a fact about your personal life (a background asset) that is at least somewhat relevant, but definitely impressive. For example, you have reached the point in the discussion where the issue becomes, "What should we do next on this project?" Since you need time to think about the real answer, you use the packaging technique of allegory: "When I was in the Eco-Challenge and we fell into quicksand, here's what we did"—playing on the fact that you got through it as a team. Suddenly, another facet of your competence emerges at the same time that a Stone Soup type of discussion erupts about "What should *we* do next?"

- **Shift strategy.** You may have gone into the discussion building layer upon layer in Pearl-like fashion, but having run out of layers, you start asking questions like an Interrogator. Just think back to the layers that people contributed and begin with, "That action could make a difference here. Can you tell me more?"

BODY LANGUAGE

- Use gestures that indicate that you're thinking as you verbally buy time.

- Use regulators to encourage someone else to talk as you think about your next move.

- Move to a different part of the room. I commonly place my water in a part of the room that's slightly away from where I'm presenting. If I need to buy time, I take a few seconds and walk to my water glass.

Sometimes swimming to safety means holding enough air to get to the sand. So, buying time with any one of these verbal or nonverbal initiatives can be the most important part of self-rescue.

That's what I relied on when my brain froze during *The Night of January 16*. I adopted the body language of someone who needed to convince each and every juror that my words should not be disputed. I boldly searched their faces, looking for acceptance, for a full 15 seconds until my memory shuffled through the stacks of lines and arrived at the right one.

CALL FOR HELP

Your allies do not have to be alerted in advance to secret hand gestures or code words to come to your rescue. In fact, in many cases, they will help you inadvertently, just by responding normally to a setup that you provide.

However you trigger the rescue, you need to know who the allies in your audience are, and whether they are natural allies or those that you've created through bonding.

Going back to my desperate situation in the play, people wanted to help me, but no one could. Normally, there are lots of ways people can help you in a tense situation—as long as they want you to stay alive. Each of the main characters in your play— the natural leader, the genuine expert, and the loud guy—has the potential to save you if you find yourself drowning during your presentation. What reason have you given him for doing so?

- **The natural leader.** In trying to solve a problem for him, maybe you're almost there. You've stopped short, but by this time, he has a vested interest in your survival for two possible reasons: First, he thinks you're on to something that will take his pain away and wants you to have the chance to complete the task, and second, his attention to you and deference to you as an expert mean that he will look like a fool if you look like a fool.

- **The genuine expert.** The way you established common ground with her, acknowledged her contributions, and listened attentively ("I hadn't thought of that!") are all ways you could have cultivated a bond that gives her an incentive to rescue you.

- **The loud guy.** Your bond with him at this point might be based on the fact that you brought him into the conversation and/or validated something he said. Unless he's a sociopath, he will not want you to drown, since you made him look good. If you drown, you drag a little bit of him down with you.

Again, the ways to call for help fall into the categories of verbal and nonverbal, and I've included some cautions here about body language that says, "I'm pathetic," rather than, "I need help."

VERBAL

- **Call for participation.** Instructors do this all the time, but you've probably thought that it's just a standard teaching technique. Professor Morgan has run out of information, so

How to Become an Expert on Anything in Two Hours

he says to the class, "I'm not sure everyone's getting this, so does anyone have any questions at this point?" Another version of this, in both the classroom and the business setting, is a question that invites interpretation: "What does that mean to you?" You're giving yourself more food for thought, and a pause while you regroup. Since you are asking people to ruminate on your subject, if you have dropped your line of thought, you will get cues that will give you the next line.

- **Highlight a point of intersecting interests.** Someone who shares a concern or point of view with you will not want to see you founder. If you do, you lose ground, and she loses ground. Reinforcing this bond often makes the person see you as an expert and want to be identified with you, so she supports you verbally, rescuing you in the process.

- **Use one of the techniques to summon aid.** Naïveté or flattery could work very well in a call for help. You may exaggerate your ignorance, for example, so that someone can help you bounce back stronger: "Those fires in Georgia are a natural occurrence, so why shouldn't they be allowed to burn themselves out?" Your rescuer might address the risk to homeowners, the economic impact on tree farming in the state, and the threat to wildlife. At that point, you could jump in with, "Good point. Peat burns for years [something you learned in your research], so if the fires reach a nearby bog, that could create a serious long-term problem for animals that wander through there."

- **Make Stone Soup.** Stone Soup is a good time filler, so for that reason alone it's a useful rescue strategy. It also provides an easy framework for people to bail you out quickly without even realizing that they're doing it. A third reason is that it is a natural way to expand the number of your allies; that is, there are suddenly more people who have jumped in as potential rescuers. The more people there are in the water, the greater your chances of making it to shore. There are two main ways to use a Stone Soup strategy for rescue:

- **Fish for facts.** I was in a meeting recently in which a female finance executive began, "I just put these slides together a few minutes ago." Most of us thought that was a setup for failure, but she quickly engaged people in fleshing out the slides and completing the presentation. It's very easy to make the transition from the question-dominated strategy of Interrogator to Stone Soup, too. When you hit a dead end in the Interrogator strategy, just turn it around and say, "I've been asking all the questions, but now let me make sure I've got everything." And then you invite people to recap their contributions and draw conclusions.

- **Ask for opinions.** Remember being in class when your teacher asked a question like, "Who do you think was the best president?" All the kids raised their hands. Maybe they repeated something their parents had said during the last election, or maybe they threw in something they'd read in a book. The teacher then took all of those opinions and asked more questions about this guy who led us through a war or that guy who united the nation in hope. Finally, the class would come to a consensus—the one that the teacher was driving it toward—that Abraham Lincoln was the best president. The class would then "taste the soup," with everyone having a sense of pride that they had all contributed to the success. The conclusion was, "My cabbage made the difference."

BODY LANGUAGE

Eye contact with an ally who knows you well may be all you need to prompt a rescue, but do not try that with someone who's sitting on the fence between acceptance and rejection or someone who could perceive your eye contact as threatening. The last thing you want is someone saying, "What's wrong, Sheila?"

- Maintain confident postures, but do not try to punctuate weak points with flailing illustrators as a way of inflating their importance. Watch C-Span's coverage of congressional hearings if you want to see this mistake in action on a daily basis. If you want to do anything, combining your confident posture with a suppliant outstretched arm to someone you've asked a question of is a subtle way to ask for help.

- Use your brows to flash recognition at the sound of a good idea as a way of encouraging someone to keep talking. But remember, recognition of a person or idea involves a momentary rise only. If you hold your brows in that position, the result is the request for approval, and you want to avoid that as much as saying out loud, "I've totally screwed this up, haven't I?" Conversely, you don't want to send the message, "What are you thinking?" as the person shares and tries to help.

DROWN THE OTHER GUY

You don't have to run faster than the bear, just faster than the guy next to you. The bear will take care of everything else.

Okay, maybe I've mixed ocean and Alpine forest metaphors now, but the point is that sometimes you need to use extreme interpersonal skills to save yourself. I don't recommend the actions in this section lightly, by the way. These should be part of your rescue scheme only in situations where your credibility has been deliberately attacked by someone who wants to see you go down. So you take him down instead. More than any other part of this book, these pieces of guidance reflect the dark side of interrogation—

manipulation. This is Machiavellian, so if you do not have the connection with it, skip over this section.

In the case of a single source of threat, here are useful actions that enable you to climb on someone else's shoulders while he drowns. You need to know your audience very well before you try any of them, however. If you execute these techniques badly or pick on the wrong person in the organization, not only will you lose the credibility you've built, but you will also look like a fool.

VERBAL

- **Use flattery quickly followed by criticism in a one-two punch.** Interrogators do this in a combination of what we call pride-and-ego up and pride-and-ego down. The person is off guard for the next move because he thinks you have started down a particular track. Most likely, he will respond in an appropriate manner, and then will have no frame of reference for responding quickly to the second half of your technique. You say, "Kip, what a great idea to install all that new scheduling software just in time for the series of fall and winter companies meetings." He replies with thanks and looks around the room to make sure that everyone has heard the wonderful thing he's done. And then you say, "Too bad Congress just changed Daylight Saving Time. Caught the computer industry off guard. They say they won't have upgrades ready for another two months."

- **Elicit strong emotion.** What you did to Kip in the previous scenario demonstrates to everyone in the room that you have manipulated him, and almost invariably, that awakens strong emotion. Let's speculate that Kip took a deep breath and managed to keep his rage inside. His plan is to return the volley with an attack that worked before: hitting you in your weak spot (which is what he did to provoke your remark in the first place). He points to the gaping hole in your knowledge of the project that you tried to demonstrate your expertise about. You return his comment with silence, a cocked head, and a quizzical look, as if to say, "I feel so sorry for you. I only wish you made sense." As I've mentioned before, most humans hate silence. Your body language needs to convey absolute confidence and pity, or else you risk looking weak and afraid. You will evoke a response—most likely, an emotional one. Whether Kip storms out of the room, raises his voice, or makes an uncomfortable joke, you have aroused enough visible emotion to take him down a notch in everyone's eyes.

- **Take him into your deep water.** Perhaps Kip is the loud guy who has plagued you from the very beginning of your presentation. At your darkest moment, when the water has risen up to your nose, use your last breath to say, "Kip has been at this a lot longer than I have; I'm going to defer to his judgment on this." In all likelihood, you have just outed him as an ignoramus, or at least reminded other people that that's what he is. Another approach is, "Kip and I can do this together," as you look at him starting to dog paddle. Often the best ploy is to take him to the edge and then rescue *him*. Although he may realize that you have caused the stress, he will be grateful that you also relieved it.

BODY LANGUAGE

- **Your composed posture needs to remain unbroken.** But feel free to accent it with those subtle expressions of disgust that you learned from your mother when she caught you about to draw on the wall. These would be aimed at your nemesis, of course. A drowning person is not the picture of control unless she wants to commit suicide, so why would anyone who sees your composure ever suspect that you are going under?

- **Selectively project vulnerability.** When I told you not to project vulnerability, I should have added a caveat: unless you want to draw someone in and then use your big gun at the last minute. If your generally composed demeanor takes on the appearance of momentary helplessness, all eyes will be on you. It's your chance to have the loud guy publicly try to shove your head under water, only to have you return his attack with a jaw-breaking blow of information.

These are dirty tricks, designed primarily for use with someone who has overtly and with malice tried to undermine your acceptance as an expert.

PRIMROSE PATH

You may face more than a single source of threat. You may have to face a room full of people who are not convinced that you know what you're talking about. The model for converting them is the kind of indoctrination exercises used by Chinese brainwashers during the Korean War. These techniques were also exported to interrogation and indoctrination officers during the Vietnam War. This distorted version of Stone Soup welcomes contributions, but sorts through the contributions to allow the soup to taste only the way you want it to—exactly. I'll focus on the Maoist style here to give you a framework for how you can manipulate someone who strongly disagrees with you to come over to your side. It is a rescue technique *par excellence* because people who had previously condemned you find themselves trapped in a position where they have to agree with you.

Your plan is to get people to believe in a key concept that's related to some principle.

A relatively easy way to begin is by educating people by asking questions that ensure that they know what you're talking about, and then using their words against them. In a rescue situation, you are setting yourself up as the ultimate expert, and setting everyone else up in such a way that they drown themselves.

The premise is that you pare the available options throughout the course of the dialogue. You throw out information to get others to validate it. You wait until you get the reaction you need in order to get your point across. Teachers do this all the time. Bosses do it all the time. They bait you until you say what they want to hear— something that idealistically agrees with them—and then they applaud your insights and move on. The effect is like following a tree limb out to a very small branch: Every decision point moves you further from the other options.

Just like those teachers, you ask people to respond to a premise. They do so, and then you choose the response you want to focus on. Allow people to throw out answers until one of them suits your needs, but remember to enforce limits. Too many answers and you look stupid and indecisive.

You structure this so that people don't know what path they're headed down. Ostensibly, you are doing nothing more than using their words to move them along down the road of logic. You cue people with questions and then let their own words pare down the options that lie before them. In effect, you reverse-engineer the conversation, starting with an intended outcome and working your way back to the point of your design. I equate this particular brand of manipulation to ducklike behavior: On the surface, you look poised and graceful; underneath the surface (or in your head, in this case), you are paddling like hell.

In my days of running interrogation exercises to train peacetime soldiers, we had large numbers of interrogators and large numbers of guards. Peacetime lacks only one thing—prisoners. In order to get prisoners, we hired role players. The problem was that all of these make-believe prisoners were also very American, real live soldiers. Their job was to go into the interrogation room spouting some anti-American rhetoric. Most of them were young Americans trained at the Defense Language Institute who had little or no frame of reference for how non-Americans see us. I needed to help them understand how people who are fed a steady regimen of anti-American sentiment feel about the United States.

I would start the meeting as a session about politics in the Middle East. My objective was to get the role players to understand how people living in an anti-American regime viewed us and our way of life. All they knew was that I had come in to help them develop a fuller understanding of America's enemies, so they had no preconceived notions about mind tricks I might use. I coopted a tool of Maoists to help these American soldiers understand the way many of our enemies view the world, and particularly view Americans, so that they could better play the role of an enemy prisoner of war.

I began with, "I want to talk with you today about how other people in the world perceive Americans. What do you think other people think of America?"

Nobody was going to say, "Fantastic!" They knew better than that. So they came up with some critical remarks like "imperialistic."

I countered them. "No. Not everybody feels that way." So I started down the road without treading on negative territory. I wanted them to think I was on their side in the beginning.

So the next round of comments wasn't so negative. I heard "wealthy," "dynamic," and other assessments that implied arrogance and greed, but didn't state that explicitly. The list grew, but it had a lot of mixed sentiments, since the trainee role players didn't know exactly where I stood.

I kept hearing their words of implied and overt criticism, integrated them into my subsequent questions, let them toss those ideas around, and then stepped away from them. They came up with their own forceful reasons why "wealthy" described Americans, for example, but didn't describe most people outside the United States, particularly America's enemies.

They came up with their own logical explanation of how a global perception of America's image of prosperity and Superman persona came to be: World War II.

"Why World War II?" I asked.

"Because we saved the world," they replied.

"People in England would disagree," I said. "They paid the ultimate price." And then I paused. "But then, there's the Pacific. We are, unarguably, the people who saved the Pacific. Right?"

They wholeheartedly agreed, until we ticked through the countries, starting with Japan, that we didn't exactly "save." The discussion moved on until the conclusion was that, without a doubt, America had saved the Philippines.

I asked when the Philippines declared independence, and someone said, "July 4, 1946." And then I took them down the path of questioning their ability to even discuss America's role in the Philippines. "Who did the Philippines gain independence from?" The United States. "So, who did the United States liberate the Philippines from?" Japan. "So, who did Japan take them from?" The United States. As we walked backwards and forwards, it became less clear who had a legitimate claim.

And then I asked the trainees what the Philippine culture was like before the country was "rescued" by America. Agrarian, they said. "What did we do for them?" was how I then began the next phase of attitude-shifting questions. Their answer: "We gave them industry." I asked, "What kind?" and a knowledge of history helped someone answer, "An organized fishing industry."

By this time, we were well down the path toward having them become full-fledged critics of American culture. I focused their attention on "organized." They got animated about how localized fishing didn't provide jobs for a lot of people and left them in poverty, but organizing gave them opportunities. I could then illustrate how these "opportunities" brought deforestation, pollution, corruption, and a loss of indigenous arts and crafts. Every defense of American cultural influence brought dissention among them—not from me—about the true benefits of "saving" the Philippines.

A Maoist indoctrination exercise like this has value to you in that you can see the path for taking people to where you want them to be. The scheme involves throwing out questions and then cherry-picking the answers to drive the discussion toward a predetermined conclusion. Each of your decision points drives you further from the alternatives. Communist indoctrinators in the USSR, China, and countless other countries have used this tactic. Never mind that the facts are not accurate and that when they are just "half truths," they are the words of the crowd. If someone attacks the words, he is attacking ingredients, not the soup itself.

If you do this well, you have to be very concerned about what you leave behind. You may produce people who are disenchanted and even plant the seeds of disrespect. The process involves the use of half truths and selective facts, adding only the ingredients that make the soup taste the way you want it to. This technique has been used by all the great reform movements of the mid-twentieth century.

FENDING OFF SHARKS

Here's one of those useless statistics that's useful right now: The chances of your dying from a shark attack are 1 in 300,000,000. My point is that your familiarity with these rescue schemes is good mental preparation, but you may never have to use them— especially the really mean ones.

True, I have watched seasoned interrogators run out of questions in the midst of a session with a source and feel like fools. But they aren't fools, and neither are you just because you find yourself needing a rescue. Your focus on this vital topic means that you deserve credit for thorough preparation and aiming for an unbroken streak of success.

The Machiavellian techniques that involve drowning others can lead you to sacrifice someone else, only to find out that he was your best ally. Instead, coopt others to help you. Insulation works better than finding high ground on someone else's shoulders.

As a final note, now that you're aware of all the things that can go right and go awry, be a good Samaritan. If you see someone else drowning, throw a rope. There is always value to saving someone else.

You never know when the rescuer will need a rescue.

UP FOR AIR

Drowning and self-preservation—feel-good topics, right?

Throughout this book, I have been dedicated to teaching you uplifting skills, not sacrificing others or pretending to be an expert. The focus has consistently been on how to take a little time to prepare well and to invest heavily in understanding the needs of others so that you can become the one who makes the information coincide with the person. If nothing else, you have learned to look for real intent and short-circuit the guy who is planning and scheming to throw you to the sharks.

Take a tip from Clint Eastwood's Dirty Harry: Put him on notice. This often works better than attempting to drown him. But when all else fails, you now have professional tools.

CONCLUSION

ARE YOU CLOSER TO THE ONE?

¤ ¤ ¤

At the very beginning of this book—on the first page of Chapter 1—I asked you to make a list of experts. Take it out now and go back over it. Would you make any changes in it? Are the experts you originally chose still on the list? Do you have any new ones, and if so, why? Do you still have any question marks in the third column?

Human experience and deference—the two are inextricably linked, regardless of whom you claim as parents, or who educated you. Those parents and educators left you with deference for people in similar roles. Do you now realize how much of the human experience involves looking for others to fill the role of expert? Turn on the news tonight and watch three analysts. Ask yourself, "Why should I let her tell me anything?" and "What has he figured out that I can't from simple research on the Internet?" and "How much of my trust in you comes from the fact that you're very good looking?"

Dig deeper as the questions mount. Pay particular attention to people's body language. Was that confidence, or was that adaptor a dead giveaway of uncertainty?

Here's something to drag into your dream state tonight: Where are the skeptics in your daily life that prevent you from being the expert? Are you the biggest skeptic in your own life? Are you the main person who blocks the door to your acceptance as an expert?

Master the messages of confidence. (Put this sentence on your computer terminal and your refrigerator.)

You now have the tools not only to determine who are experts and when they are truly confident, but also to be an expert yourself.

As you think about the topic that drove you to pick up this book, think about the audience for your expertise. Is the audience sophisticated? Compared to your current understanding, or your old one? Your audience will always be the driving force behind everything you do in this realm, from choice of language, to depth of research, to what you are trying to achieve.

So if you picked up this book as a route to impressing your friends and associates with how adeptly you could move from topic to topic—the Renaissance man come alive in the office—remember that the best source of expertise is often those people that you are trying to impress. Expertise comes in all shapes and sizes, and the gem you seek just might be "Bob in the mailroom." Make Stone Soup with him one afternoon and see if it tastes good.

If you picked up this book to get ahead at work, obviously your audience is different from prospective dates, and what you need to accomplish will be different as well. Regardless of the different intended outcomes, though, the modus operandi is still making a connection. Always pay attention to the roles and motivation of the people you are engaging.

As you start your two hours of research, look at what it is you truly want to achieve. Resist the temptation to follow the white rabbit down the hole in pursuit of information. Diving down the hole may be fun for a moment, but it's a lot like leaving the airplane with no parachute (i.e., with no plan for survival). You always need to keep in mind the three criteria for directed research that creates real expertise: audience, outcome, and duration. By determining how long you have to maintain your expertise, who your intended audience is, and what you intend to get from this session, you will conduct directed research that gives you what you need in order to present information that intersects with people.

Our last big message is a reprise:

A human being should be able to change a diaper, plan an invasion, butcher a hog, conn a ship, design a building, write a sonnet, balance accounts, build a wall, set a bone, comfort the dying, take orders, give orders, cooperate, act alone, solve equations, analyze a new problem, pitch manure, program a computer, cook a tasty meal, fight efficiently, die gallantly. Specialization is for insects.

—Robert A. Heinlein, science fiction author,
in *Time Enough for Love*

Replay the Heinlein quote in your mind as you refer back to bits of advice throughout the book. Specialization is for insects. But if you have to specialize in something, make it human beings. What you are doing is building a base of understanding of how to apply information to the human condition. Once you do this, you can move from topic to topic and rely on the fact collectors to build on your limited understanding to create a pearl from a grain of sand.

APPENDIX: WISDOM OF THE AGES

Proverbs hang around for generation after generation for a good reason: They have withstood the test of time. So, I'm going to give you 15 pieces of great-grandma wisdom from several cultures that offer the basic rules of good planning and preparation, as well as tips on how to apply these well.

If you believe everything you read, better not read. (Japanese proverb)

Some people seem convinced that the modern world would not have a problem with misinformation if it weren't for technology, but there have always been snake-oil salesmen and gossipy neighbors. Human beings need to cultivate a healthy level of skepticism. When they don't, people like Hitler have an easy time taking over.

If you take big paces, you leave big spaces. (Burmese proverb)

This can serve as a reminder that the framework for your research will affect your trail of conversation. If you cover a lot of ground because you want the big picture, and you plan to use a strategy to get others to fill in the details, then just be mindful of the big spaces.

If it sounds too good to be true, it probably is. (Unknown source)

Ads for gadgets and self-help books that are "guaranteed" to change your life should make you laugh, not get you to spend

$19.95 a month for the next three years. You do not want to use any version of this in presenting yourself as an expert, so stay away from research sources that use it.

In baiting a mousetrap with cheese, always leave room for the mouse. (Greek proverb)

Chapter 9 explores the topic of when to shut up, but this is a good introduction to it. If you keep putting out information, never letting anyone get closer to you through the give and take of conversation, you will blow opportunities to gain acceptance as an expert. Bait your audience with well-placed bits of information, and then let a conversation unfold.

It takes time to build castles. Rome was not built in a day. (Irish proverb)

Really smart people know that they will not gain in-depth knowledge of a subject in two hours, unless it's something simple like assembling shelves from Ikea. Use of a strategy like the Pearl allows you to build on your knowledge throughout the entire duration of your meeting, even if it's an all-day job interview.

Life is a bridge. Cross over it, but build no house on it. (Indian proverb)

Some information is nothing more than the link that gets you from one major concept to another. For example, if you want to learn what's involved in replacing a roof, you want to consider materials, square feet, pitch, configuration, and other elements that affect the difficulty and cost of roofing. You wouldn't spend 15 minutes of the hour you've devoted to this research focusing on the fact that reroofing can damage your rain gutters. That's good to know, but you need to move on.

Live with wolves, and you learn to howl. (Spanish proverb)

Have you ever been at a meeting where people got so emotional about their positions that they sounded more like wild animals than business executives? People in meetings sometimes unwittingly give others around them permission to forgo decorum. In that case, your strongest demonstration of expertise may just be to excuse yourself. Your research and strategies give you the ability to display expertise to creatures with cognitive abilities; don't bother to learn how to howl.

One flower will not make a garland. (French proverb)

One detail or piece of jargon does not make you an expert. Neither will just two or three strung together.

Only the wearer knows where the shoe pinches. (English proverb)

Even when you know you've hit a discussion area where you're vulnerable, rely on the body language of a confident person who is on the road to gaining acceptance as an expert. Do not make it obvious that someone has just hit your sore spot.

Pigs might fly, but they are most unlikely birds. (Unknown source)

You have to know where to draw the line in presenting yourself as an expert. The first rule is to be authentic, and your research will help you a great deal in defining the limits of "authentic." Do not pretend that you're the pope's aide or the president's chef. Even if you think you know all about the pope's habits or the president's diet, by playing a role like that, you will invite personal questions that will immediately erode your credibility.

Roasted pigeons will not fly into one's mouth. (Dutch proverb)

Planning and preparation are all about putting together the raw ingredients you need to create a finished "product." Again, data from the mouth of an autistic savant demonstrate no expertise, but processing those data, packaging them, and delivering them in a way that makes them appealing to your audience will lead to success.

The beginning of wisdom is to call things by their right names. (Chinese proverb)

A friend of mine is a business consultant who skydives, and he finds that people in meetings frequently try to connect with him by chatting about skydiving. "I hear you're a sky jumper," they begin. (The word is *skydiver*.) "Did you dive last weekend?" is another question he hears a lot. (It's *jump*.) Another common mistake is to refer to him as a "parachute jumper." If you do a search on that term on the Web, you will definitely find it in newspaper articles written by "whuffos" (short for people who ask, "What for you jump out of a perfectly good airplane?"). The research point here, once again, is to know your audience. Learn your nomenclature from sources that speak his language, not from third-party sources that have had a quick brush with the information.

The girl who can't dance says the band can't play. (Yiddish proverb)

Using any tactic to attack someone will backfire if you're the one who is not adept with the information.

There are many paths to the top of the mountain, but the view is always the same. (Chinese proverb)

Five people in a meeting might be contributing five different plans for achieving the company's sales goal. You emerge as a coalition builder—a very valuable type of expert—when you keep people mindful of the goal and interested in finding the best way to get there, rather than clinging to their plan as the only way to get there. Your research and knowledge base steer the discussion; they don't dominate it.

What belongs to everybody belongs to nobody. (Spanish proverb)

If you throw out common knowledge as expertise, it isn't.

GLOSSARY

Adaptation—One of the 8 ways to set yourself up as an expert

Adaptors—Gestures to release stress and to adjust the body as a way to increase the comfort level

Affiliation—One of the 8 ways to set yourself up as an expert

Allegory—One of the 5 principles to make correlations and to eliminate complexities that can get in the way of understanding core concepts

Approaches—Psychological techniques of persuasion used by interrogators

Association—One of the 8 ways to set yourself up as an expert

Barriers—Postures and gestures we use when we are uncomfortable

Baselining—Determining how a person behaves and speaks under normal circumstances

Christmas Tree—One of the 5 principles to make correlations and to eliminate complexities that can get in the way of understanding core concepts

Demonstration—One of the 8 ways to set yourself up as an expert

Expertise—The intersection of information and human requirements

Families of information—One of the 5 principles to make correlations and to eliminate complexities that can get in the way of understanding core concepts

Generalization—One of the 8 ways to set yourself up as an expert

Humanizing—One of the 8 ways to set yourself up as an expert

Illustrators—Gestures used to punctuate a statement

Interpreter—One of the 6 strategies to manage information so that you exhibit expertise

Interrogator—One of the 6 strategies to manage information so that you exhibit expertise

Intimidation—One of the 8 ways to set yourself up as an expert

Isolation—One of the 8 ways to set yourself up as an expert

Parsing—One of the 5 principles to make correlations and to eliminate complexities that can get in the way of understanding core concepts

Pearl—One of the 6 strategies to manage information so that you exhibit expertise

Refiner—One of the 6 strategies to manage information so that you exhibit expertise

Regulators—Gestures used to control another person's speech

Rules of Thumb—One of the 5 principles to make correlations and to eliminate complexities that can get in the way of understanding core concepts

Spider—One of the 6 strategies to manage information so that you exhibit expertise

Stone Soup—One of the 6 strategies to manage information so that you exhibit expertise

Index

eyebrow flash, 50, 220
eyebrow movement, 49–51

face, 49–52
false cognates, 141–142
flattery, 181, 218
    with criticism, 221
    to get people to talk, 120
focus
    of audience, 80
    lack of, 65
    in mood analysis, 63
fragmentation, of fields of study, 19
frame of reference, 134
framework, 160–161
futility, 120, 181

gain, potential, as motivator, 85–86
generalist personality, 95–96
generalization, 24
genuine expert, 35, 36, 217
    options for gaining trust, 37
gestures, 45, 215
God-centric expertise, 16
good manager, 3
Graham, Benjamin, 32–33
grief muscle, 50
The Guantanamo Guidebook, 172–173
guilds, 17

hands, 53
Hastings, David, 160
Heinlein, Robert A., 20
help
    call for, 216–220
    for others, 228
helplessness, body language of, 69
heretic, 15
Holt, Jim, 32
holy people, offspring, 16–19

honesty, 121
human behavior, basic understand-
    ing of, 26
humanizing, 24–25
humor, self-deprecating, 213–214

ignorance, 181
    exaggerating, 218
    to get people to talk, 121
illustrators in body language, 45–
    46, 70–71
    for acceptance, 57
    for projection, 73–74
    for rejection, 60
    for undecided, 59
incentives, 181
    to get people to talk, 119
indoctrination exercises, 223–227
infidel, 15
information
    anomalies in, 138–139
    false cognates, 141–142
    families of, 154–156
    matching with audience,
        130–132
    overload, 149–150
    priority, 132–135
    rules of thumb for anchoring,
        159
    running out of, 196–197
    sensing approach to gathering,
        161
    simplicity/complexity, 139–141
    types, 97–100
    validation by others, 224
Information Age, 21
intelligence map, 87
internal voice, 48
interpreter strategy, 106–107, 176
    inept vs. adept, 116–117